ABSTRACTS

form the

COUNTY COURT MINUTE BOOK OF

Culpeper County

Virginia

1763-1764

Compiled by

A. M. PRICHARD

Staunton, Va.

Southern Historical Press
Greenville, South Carolina

Please direct all correspondence and orders to:

www.southernhistoricalpress.com
or
SOUTHERN HISTORICAL PRESS, Inc.
PO BOX 1267
Greenville, SC   29601
southernhistoricalpress@gmail.com

Originally published: Dayton, VA. 1930
ISBN #0-89308-792-0
All rights Reserved.
Printed in the United States of America

Until the Summer of 1929, when the County Court Minute Book of 1763 of the County Court of Culpeper County, Virginia, was discovered in an old residence in Culpeper, Va., there were, for many years, no pre-revolutionary court minute books in the clerk's office of Culpeper County, and this is the only one now available. The first 270 pages of it are missing, and the balance is badly mutilated.

Preface

For many years there has been some confusion with reference to the exact date that Culpeper was made a county. On page 160 of Part II, of Green's Notes to St. Mark's Parish, it is said: "The earliest county court held for Culpeper County, as shown by the deed books, the first minute book having been lost, was on the 18th day of May, 1749, without the place being mentioned." At the bottom of page 211, Vol. VI, Henining's Statutes At Large, among the Private Acts, appears the title of "An Act for dividing the county of Orange." The General Assembly at which this act was passed began its sessions on the 27th day of October, 1748, as shown at page 408, Vol. V., Henning's Statutes At Large. A copy of the foregoing act, taken from the records in England, is as follows:

"For the greater ease and convenience of the inhabitants of the County of Orange in attending courts and other public meetings Be it Enacted by the Lieutenant Governor, Council and Burgesses of this present General Assembly, and it is hereby enacted by the Authority of the same that from and immediately after the seventeenth day of May next ensuing the said County of Orange shall be divided into two counties that is to say all that part of the County lying on the south side of Rappahanock River to the head of the Conway River shall be one distinct county and retain the name of Orange County, and all that other part thereof on the north side of the said Rappahanock and Conway River commonly called the Fork of Rappanahock River shall be one other distinct County and called and known by the name of Culpeper County; and that for the due administration of justice after the said seventeenth day of May a court for the said County of Orange be constantly held by the justices thereof upon the fourth Thursday, and a court for the said County of Culpeper be constantly held by the justices thereof upon the third Thursday of every month in such manner as by the laws of this Colony is provided and shall be by their Commissions directed Provided always that nothing herein contained shall be construed to hinder the sherif or collector of the said County of Orange as the same now stands entire and undivided to make Distress for any levies fees or dues which shall be due from the said

County of Culpeper after the said seventeenth day of May in such manner and not otherwise as by law he might have done if this act had never been made, any law, custom or usage to the contrary thereof notwithstanding.

March 22, 1748, Read the third time & passed the House of Burgesses.

PETER RANDOLPH, C. H. B.

March 23, 1748, Read the 3rd time & agreed to by the Council.

N. WALTHOE, C. G. A.

WILLIAM GOOCH

JOHN RORINSON, Speaker

A Copy Test, William Randolph, C. H. B."

NOTE by the Compiler.

The old style, or Julien, calendar was the official calendar of Great Brittain and her colonies until after the year 1751; and, according to that calendar, each new year began on the 25th day of March; so the year 1749 began just two days after the Council agreed to the foregoing act, which provided that Culpeper County should come into existence immediately after the 17th day of May next ensuing its passage. The birthday of Culpeper County, therefore, was beyond question the 18th day of May, 1749.

Abstracts, Culpeper County, Virginia

William Green—county lieutenant of militia.

Deed from Henry Elly & Esther, his wife, & ————Elly & Claria, his wife to Jeremiah Sims, rec'd.

Richard Gaines app't'd road surveyor in place of Ja———— McDaniel.

Michael Smith et als petition for road to the Dutch Church through plantation of Harrensparger's dec'd. Ordered that James Barbour, Ell———— Bohannon, William Walker & Ephraim Rucker view & report.

William Brown, John Brown, James Rucker, Ephraim Rucker & John Slaughter appointed captains of militia under William Green county lieutenant.

John Lawler took oath as deputy under William Green sheriff. Court adjourned. Minutes signed by Ambrose Powell. 17 March 1763.

Court convened. Present justices: Robert Green, William Williams, Benjamin Roberts, James Slaughter & Henry Field Jr., Gent.

Grand jury called for 3rd Thursday in May next.

Peter Clore's will exhibited by John Clore & John Yeager, ex'rs; proved by Samuel Klugg, Nicholas Cri———— & Michael Leatherer, witnesses. Ex'rs declining to act, the court app'ted Barbara Clore, Widow, admrx. Appraisers: James Barbour Jr., Adam Wayland, Henry Ayler & George Holt.

Thomas Robinson qualified to practice law, his license being signed b yJohn Randolph, George Wythe & Robert Carter.

Deed from Francis Tyler to John Yancey, recorded.

William Pritchett appointed road surveyor from his house & from Richard Rennold's to road near the widow Johnston's.

Deed Francis Yates & Ann, his wife, to George Kinnaird,

acknowledged and recorded.

Ditto Charles Yancy & Elizabeth, his wife to John Yancy.

Ditto Ambrose Powell & Mary his wife to William Bledsoe & Elizabeth his wife, & Mumford Stephens.

Ditto. Mortgage William Baker to George Strother.

Deed of gift Robert Freeman to Hugh Freeman proved by William Eastham & Dickie Latham witnesses.

Page (275)

Will of John Wetherall proved by James Strother, Mary Morris & Philip Clayton; witnesses. Ex'rs named—George Wetherall, Nathaniel Pendleton, & William Williams, refusing to act, court appointed Margaret Wetherall, widow admx., and James Strother, French Strother, Reuben Long & Robert Coleman appraisers.

Deed Timothy Swindell & Rebecca, his wife, to Michael Swindell, ackgd & recd.

Bond from James Kirtley to Margaret Kirtley recd. Will of Francis Kirtley exhibited by William Kirtley Thomas Kirtley & Francis Kirtley, exrs.; proved by Richard Guffin, John Hume, Benjamin James & James ————, witnesses.

Page (276)

Will of Michael Clore exhibited by John Clore exor.; proved by George Row & Christopher Crigler, witnesses. Elizabeth, widow, renounced benefits of the will; & James Barbour, Adam Wayland, Henry Ayler, & George Holt appointed appraisers.

George Kinnaird licensed to keep an ordinary at forks of Finleson's road below the church.

Motion of George Wetherall showing that his father John Wetherall, decd., bequeathed 400 acres of land to be equally divided between himself & his brother John, an infant; ordered that Nathaniel Pendleton represent the infant.

Page (277)

Petition of Lewis Davis Yancy to turn road, ordered that Capt. Francis Slaughter, Thomas Covington, William Slaughter & John Favor view & report.

John Flint exempted from payment of county levies.

John Campbell vs. Benjamin Hawkins—On suggestion that

Robert Gray, a witness, was about to leave the Colony, ordered that his deposition be taken.

John, Elizabeth & Barbara, children of John Daniel Jacobi, chose their father as their guardian.

Power of atty John Daniel Jacobi to his son John F.———— Lucas Jacobi, ackgd & recd.

Certificate of ages of John, Elizabeth, Barbara & Daniel, children of John Daniel Jacobi, ehxibited.

Page (278)

William Eastham & George Wetherall took oath as justices of the peace.

George Goggans appointed constable in place of Job Popham.

Inventory of John Rogers, decd, recd.

Report of William Staunton et als, viewers, on road from Joseph Edens returned.

Alexander McDaniel appointed constable in place of Isaac Norman.

18 March 1763.

Present: Ambrose Powell, William Williams, John Slaughter & William Eastham, justices.

William Roberts v. ————. Execution against Lewis Stevens ordered.

Page (279)

William Pannill gdn of Pannill's orphans ordered to render an account.

John Strother, orphan of James Strother, decd, & Ward of French Strother, his brother, being of lawful age, his guardian is discharged.

Administration of John Harrensparger's Est. cont'd. Petition of Joseph Eddins for road dismissed.

Motion of Charles Linch to fine John Biggs for failure to appear as witness, dismissed.

Sales acc't of John Harrison's Est., ret'd.

Petition of John & Robert Cave for their part of their father's estate, dismissed.

Summons awarded against Herman Young, John Nixon,

George Dillard, Christopher Hoomes, Thomas Ballard & Andrew Kannady for tending seconds of tobacco.

Abraham Blewbaker v. William Oneal. Continued.

Page (280)

William Pinkard v. Zachary Petty. Cont'd.

Charles Lewis v. George Porter. Plea & Cont'd.

Indictment against Thomas Slaughter, John Field, Philemon Kavanaugh & Birkett Davenport.

Nathaniel Pendleton v. Henry Boughan. Dismissed.

Thomas Langdon y. John Smith. Continued.

Page (281)

Suit abated by death of Charles Kavanaugh.

Joseph James & Martin Dewitt v. Beaumont Sutton. Cont'd.

Joseph Stevens v. William Lightfoot. Cont'd.

William Green v. Thomas Yates. Cont'd.

John Latham v. John Shackleford. Cont'd.

Robert Duncanson v. John Hansford. Cont'd.

William Perfect v. Benjamin Hughes. Cont'd.

William Crawford Jr. v. Thomas Hopper. Cont'd.

Page (282)

Charles Dick v. David Ross. Attachment awarded.

John Elliott Payne v. William Robertson. Dismissed.

Thomas Scott & Joseph Wood took oath as justices.

John Yancey v. Jacob Kindrick & William Green. Pleading.

Page (283)

Thomas Grayson v. Richard Parks. Cont'd.

William Detherage v. James McDaniel. Plea & Cont'd.

Will of Humphrey Brooke proved by Elizabeth Taliaferro. Richard Brooke appointed exor. Robert Brooke, brother & heir at law of decedent summoned to contest the will. Richard Tutt, James Tutt, Thomas Minor & Thomas Fox appointed appraisers.

Joseph Wood & John Slaughter appointed coroners.

Page (284)

Power of Atty Theobald Fite & Hannah ——— wife to John Francis Lucas Jacobi, ackgd.

Valentine Seveire v. Daniel Boon. Cont'd.

William Bradley, assignee, v. William Rumsey. Plurius capias ordered.

Lenox & Scott v. Willim Nalle. Summons awarded against Benjamin Roberts, garnishee.

James Hammitt v. William Nalle. Cont'd.

John Campbell v. Benjamin Hawkins. Plea & Cont'd.

John Glassford v. Henry Curtis. Dismissed.

Page (285)

Nathaniel Pendleton v. James Hawkins. Cont'd.
Michael Thomas v. Christian Franks. Plea & Cont'd.
Oliver Towles v. Valentine Morgan. Judgt for Plff.
Lenox & Scott v. John Bernnyfell. Plff arrested, cont'd for judgt against sureties: Richard Thomas, James Graves, & John Parks.

Anthony McKettrick & Co. v. Martin Attwood. Dismissed.

Francis Slaughter, the younger, v. John Latham. Dft. gave security: William Eastham & Edward Bush.

Page (286)

James Crawford v. Francis Moore Jr. Judgt for Plff.
Findley Morroson v. William Underwood & Eleanor his wife, ex'ix of Thomas Stubblefield, decd. Cont'd.
Alexander Waugh v. Salis Hansford. Dismissed.
John Wetherall v. Samuel Moore. Abated by death of Plff.
Thomas Threlkeld v. Gabriel Jones. Cont'd.
Anthony McKittrick v. William Robertson, Judgt for Plff.

Page (287)

John Grayson v. William Grayson, James Stevens, John Wallis & George Wetherall. Continued.
John Grayson v. James Shackleford & Alice, his wife. Continued.
Thomas Withers v. William Eastham. Judgt for Plff. against dft & security, Daniel Brown.
Charles Linch v. Malcum McMurry. Continued.
Nathaniel Pendleton v. John Baker Turner. Judgt.

Page (288)

William Williams v. William Nalle & Rachell Halloway. Dismissed.

Reuben Long v. William Tutt. Judgment against garnishee: Hugh Freeman & James Slaughter.

Anthony McKettrick v. William Tutt, Judgt against Hugh Freeman, garnishee.

Page (289)

Nathaniel Pendleton, Daniel Brown, William Williams, & Benjamin Roberts ordered to let the building of porch & railing at court house.

James Ross v. John Dickerson. Attachment executed in hands of John Brown. Cont'd.

John Wallis v. John Cock. Dismissed.
William Eastham v. Samuel Kersey. Judgt for Plff.
John Benger v. Richard Scales. Dft. surrendered & discharged his security: Ambrose Camp.

Page (290)

19 March 1763.

Present: Nathaniel Pendleton, Daniel Brown, Robert Green & Henry Pendleton. Gent.

Lenox & Scott v. Richard Price. Judgt for Plff.
Robert & Thomas Dunlops v. Charles Seale. Judgt for Plff.

Page (291)

Anthony McKettrick & Co. v. Benjamin Davis. Judgt.

James Pendleton, late sheriff, v. William Eastham, Henry Pendleton, Thomas Slaughter, Robert Freeman, John Williams & Stephen Jett. Continued.

Page (292)

Roger Dixon v. William Lightfoot. Judgt for Plff.
James Barbour Jr. v. Archibald Gillison. Judgt for Plff.
John Greenfield v. William Meldrum. Judgt for Plff.
Anthony McKettrick & Co. v. John Latham. Judgt for Plff.

Page (293)

Anthony McKettrick & Co. v. John McQueen. Judgt for Plff.

John Tutt v. Francis Slaughter, the younger. Judgt.
Thomas McNeale v. James Shackleford. Judgt for Plff.

Page (294)

Anthony McKettrick & Co. v. Benjamin Davis. Cont'd.
Joseph Holtsclaw v. James Hammitt. Judgt for Plff.

William Love, assignee, v. William Roberts & Jacob Kendrick. Judgt for Plf.

Peter Lehew v. William Rice. Cont'd.
Cuthbert Bullitt v. James Ross. Judgt for Plf.
William Head v. Gabriel Amiss. Dismissed.

Page (295)

Anthony Strother v. William Rumsey. Cont'd.
Andrew Kennady & John Gressell, Admrs of Robert Burgess, decd., v. James Head. Judgt for Plf.

Thomas Athrop v. Jacob Nalle. Dismissed.

Robert Armour v. William Baker. Judgt for Plf.
Richard Vernon v. Richard Winslow. Process awarded.
David Chester v. William Tutt. Judgt for Plf.

Page (296)

James & William Knox v. Ambrose George. Dismissed.
David Harris v. William Baker. Judgt for Plf.

Elliott Bohannon v. Philemon Kavanaugh. Cont'd.
John Stewart v. John Leavell. Judgt for Plf.

Page (297)

William Gale v. William Field. Cont'd.
William Gale v. Silas Hansford. Dismissed.
William Gale v. Richard Yancey. Alias capias ordered.
Lenox v. Scott v. Benjamin Hoomes. Cont'd.
Benjamin Davis v. George McNeale. Cont'd.
David Vawter v. Samuel Young. Cont'd.
Oliver Towles v. Felix Gilbert. Dismissed agreed.

Page (298)

Cornelius Mitchell v. Edwin Hickman. Dismissed agreed.
Edward Bush v. Benjamin Davis. Continued.

John Barnes v. William Turner. Process awarded.
Thomas Edgehill v. James Barker. Dismissed agreed.
David Vawter v. Richard Stanton. Cont'd.
William Walker v. David Thompson. Process awarded.

Page (299)

John Hoard v. John Latham.   Dismissed agreed.

Edward Bush v. John Connor.   Cont'd.

William Russell v. Richard Doggett.   Cont'd with William Ball security for dft.

William Stringfellow v. John Yeoman.   Cont'd.

Francis Brown v. Alexander Frazier.   Dismissed agreed.

Thomas Aubry v. Benjamin Roberts Jr.   Dismissed.

Page (300)

John Boots v. Robert Middleton & Fra. Walle.   Cont'd.

Anthony McKettrick & Co. v. John Dickerson.   Process ordered.

Abbott White v. William Nalle.   Process awarded.

John Strother v. Henry Gambill.   Dismissed agreed.

Lewis Yancey v. William Davis.   Process awarded.

Lewis Wallis v. Oliver Small & Garfield Brown.   Process.

Page (301)

David Miller v. William Oneale.   Process awarded.

James Hammitt v. Thomas Hutchins.   Dismissed.

John Latham v. Neale McCawley.   Dismissed agreed.

Nathaniel Pendleton v. Ephriam Hubbard.   Continued.

John Strother v. Henry Gambill.   Continued with Benjamin Gambill, security.

James Buchannan v. William Lightfoot.   Continued.

Page (302)

Benjamin Pendleton v. Walter Shropshire.   Continued.

John & William Knox v. William Tutt.   Process awarded.

Allan Raines v. Richard Thomas.   Continued.

George Row, assignee of Jacob Lipham, v. William Oneale. Judgt for Plf.

Thomas Edghill v. Benjamin Gambill.   Judgt for Plf.

Page (303)

Thomas Slaughter v. William Morgan.   Dismissed.

George Prow v. John Kelly.   Continued.

William Gosney v. Beaumont Sutton.   Continued.

Birkett Davenport v. John Shropshire.   Continued with William Dewitt, security.

Church wardens of Brumfield Parish ordered to apprentice

out William Rawlins, son of John Rawlins, to Lodowick Fisher to learn trade of cardwainer.

Page (304)

John Benger v. Richard Scales. Continued with Nathaniel Pendleton & Edward Bush, security.

Lettice Stanton suggested that her husband, Thomas Stanton intended to leave the Colony & refuse her separate maintenance, & that she is obliged to live apart from him because of his inhuman & tyranical treatment, and that he cohabits in adultry with one Elizabeth Gerrard of this county. Attachment ordered.

Page (305)

21 April 1763.

Present: Daniel Brown, Robert Green, John Slaughter, Henry Pendleton & James Slaughter. Gent.

Deed relinquishing dower from Margaret Oneale & Michael Oneale to John Clore; proved by Stephen Fisher, Michael Leather & William Chapman.

Inventory of Michael Clore's Estate recd.

Gerrald Banks appointed road surveyor in place of Simon Miller.

Page (306)

Deed from William Hammitt to William Hammitt, his father.

Michael Sloane licensed to keep an ordinary.

Petition of Lewis Davis Yancey to turn road. Granted.

Charles Kavanaugh given leave to turn road.

Thomas Pratt, James Shearer & John Weekley ordered to work road under Benjamin Thomas, overseer.

Roger Oxford's exrs refused to accept burden.

David Davis appointed constable in place of George Goggins.

William White appointed constable in place of Alexander McDaniel.

Page (307)

Will of Matthias Blankenbeker proved by witnesses, and John Blankenbeker appointed admr., with Ambrose Bohannon, Henry Ayler, George Holt, & George Utz, appraisers.

Deed Benjamin Watts to John Watts proved by Benjamin Cave.

Anthony McKettrick & Co. v. Benjamin Davis. Dft gave Alexander Hawkins, security.

Deed George Utz to Mary Blankenbaker & John Blankenbeker, recorded.

Christopher Lyrle appointed admr. or Christian Reapman.

Page (308)

Joseph James licensed to keep an ordinary.

On motion of James Frinnie to turn road, Elliott Bohannon, William Booten, William Price & William Walker ordered to view & report.

Inventory of Est. of John Wetherall recd.

John Hammonds v. John McGannum. Dismissed agreed.

John Daniel Jacobi v. Samuel Moore. Dismissed agreed.

Henry Field Jr. ordered to list titables in precinct covered by Robert Green last year.

James Slaughter ordered to list titables in precinct covered by Williams last year.

Nathaniel Pendleton ordered to list titables in precinct covered by Daniel Brown last year.

Joseph Wood ordered to list titables in the fork of Robinson, Brumfield Parish.

George Wetherall ordered to list titables between Robinson & Hazel rivers.

John Slaughter ordered to list titables in precinct covered by John Strother last year.

Page (309)

Inventory of Est. of Francis Kirtley recorded.

Robert Duncanson v. John Hansford. Judgt for Plf.

Nathaniel Pendleton licensed to keep an ordinary.

Deed William Poe & Lydia, his wife, to James Buchannan, proved by John Lewis, Joseph Jones & Robert Green.

Page (310)

William Pannill, guardian of the orphans of William Pannill, decd, made report.

Anthony Strother v. William Rumsey. Continued.

John McGannon licensed to keep an ordinary.

John Gray & Co. v. William Harper. Judgt against Dft. and David Yancey, security.

Page (311)

22 April 1763.

Present: Daniel Brown, William Williams, William Kirtley & Henry Field Jr. Gent.

John Daniel Jacobi v. William Pritchett & William Frogg. Continued.

John McAllister v. Charles McQueen. Continued.

John Barrow, Exr of William Kelly v. William Morgan. Dismissed. Dft no inhabitant.

George Roberts Jr. & Catherine, his wife, v. William Russell. Continued.

Page (312)

Benjamin Hoomes v. Francis Prior. Continued.
David Johnson v. Adam Campbell. Continued.

Page (313)

Frazier & Wright v. Jacob Kendrick. Process awarded.
Ditto   v. Richard Davidson.   Ditto.

Reuben Slaughter v. John Faver & Thomas Covington. Cont'd.

Joseph Blackwell v. John & William Crawford Jr. Cont'd.
James Walker, Assignee of William Walker v. David Vawter, James Rucker & Ephriam Rucker. Judgt for Plf.

Page (314)

Andrew Cockran & Co. v James Story. Cont'd.
Ditto   v. Martin Baker. Process awarded.
Lettice Stanton by Adam Banks, next friend, v. Thomas Stanton. Continued.

Page (315)

Lenox & Scott v. William Edwards. Cont'd.
Richard Lewis v. William Brown. Cont'd.
John Lindsey v. William Meldrum, Clerk. Trial by jury as

follows: William Watkins, Joseph James, John Clayton, John Yancey, Anthony Foster, William Hansford, Oliver Towles, John Yeoman, John Creal, John Bartley, John Poe & Benjamin Hughes. Judgt for Plf.

Moles Smith, witness allowed 215 lbs. tobacco coming to and from Frederick County.

George Nicholson, witness for John Lindsey, allowed 215 lbs. tobo. to & from Fred'k County.

Report of viewers of road from Cornelius Mitchell's to county line, continued.

William Green v. Thomas Yates. Garnishee.

Page (316)

Frederick Zimmerman, discharged.

Petition of Elizabeth Clore for dower in her husband, Michael Clore's estate considered; and Ambrose Powell, James Barbour Jr., William Kirtley & George Wetherall ordered to allot said dower.

James Gaines Jr. v. William Brown.   Cont'd.

Henry Brinker v. William Meldrum, Clerk.   Cont'd.

Page (317)

Philemon Kavanaugh v. Henry Pendleton, & James Pendleton, exrs. of James Pendleton, decd.   Cont'd.

James Penny, assignee of John Pickett v. Jacob Walle & William Holloway.   Daniel Mooring became surety.

Dekar Thompson v. Thomas Hopper.   Judgt for Plf.
William Ellzy v. James Head.   Judgt for Plf.

Page (318)

William Oneal v. Michael Thomas.   Dismissed agreed.
John Roane v. James Stuart.   Dismissed agreed.
Martin Pickett v. Stephen Bailey.   Dismissed agreed.
Lettice Stanton v. Thomas Stanton.   Cont'd.

Jacob Walle & Nanny, his wife, v. Samuel Kersey & Eleanor, his wife.   Cont'd.

William Thomas & Francis Kirtley, exrs of Francis Kirtley, decd, v. John Mayfield.   Dismissed agreed.

John Shackleford v. James Hammitt.   Cont'd.

Robert Coleman v. William Tutt. Judgt against Richard Tutt, garnishee.

Page (319)

Thomas Underwood v. James Hammitt. Cont'd.

William Turner v. Joseph Gaines. Cont'd.

On suggestion of Henry Pendleton, ordered that John & Evan, poor children of Evan Thomas be apprenticed.

John Rawson appointed road surveyor in place of Archibald Gillison.

Samuel Moore v. John & Robert Gouges, Ejectment tried before the following jury:

Edward watkins, Joseph James, John Clayton, Lewis Yancey, William Hansford, John Bartley, Ambrose Camp, Richard Pollard, French Strother, Richard Yancey, Reuben Long & Richard Vernon. Judgt for Plf.

Courtney Norman allowed to turn road.

Page (320)

Benjamin Roberts Jr. witness for Samuel Moore, allowed 225 lbs. tobo. for 9 days attendance.

William Johnston Jr., witness for Samuel Moore, allowed 225 lbs. tobo. for 9 days attendance.

Cornelius Mitchell, witness for same, allowed 150 lbs. tobo. for 6 days.

Courtney Norman, witness for John & Robert Gouges, allowed 125 lbs. tobo. for 5 days.

David Johnston, witness for same, allowed 200 lbs. tobo. for 8 days.

Page (321)

Wednesday, 11 May 1763.

Present: Robert Green, William Williams, John Slaughter, Henry Pendleton & Daniel Brown.

John Daniel Jacobi acquitted.

Claim of John Barbee, for taking up negro, Tom, belonging to Colo. Hunter, certified to Gen. Assembly.

Claim of William Cramore for taking up Stephen Brown, urnaway servant of John Willis, certified.

Page (322)

19 May 1763.

- Present: Ambrose Powell, Robert Green, Henry Pendleton & Benjamin Roberts.

Alexander Woodroe & John Nielson, v. Reuben Pain. Judgment for plaintiffs.

Petition of William Robertson to have their ancient Rawling way and Church way established; ordered that James Spilman, Christopher Hutchins, John Barbee & John Read view & report.

Page (323)

- Deed Frederick Fishback & Eve, his wife, ———— Kamper & Elizabeth, his wife to John Kamper, recd.

On viewers report leave granted Michael Smith et als for road from Tevalt Christers to the Dutch Church through the plantation of John Harrensparger, decd.

David Miller v. William Oneal. Dismissed agreed.

John Corbin renewed his ordinary license.

Grand jury sworn in, viz: John Latham, foreman, William Walker, John Manifee, Jonas Manifee, John Cooper, William Smith, Nicholas Browning, Isaac Walle, Raleigh Duncan, Christopher Hoomes, Edward Price, William Robertson, John Lear, John Asher, James Stewart & Charles Stewart, made the following presentments:

Harrison Monday for prophanely swearing.

John Cheek & Catherine Omash for adultery.

James Pollard & Martha Howell for fornication.

James Brown, son of Garfield Brown, for common swearing.

Page (324)

Thomas Murphy for not going to church for 4 months.

Samuel Kersey & Hugh Freeman, true bill.

Ann Pannill to William Pannill. Release of dower.

William Pannill to Ann Pannill. Release of slaves.

Mary Martin, a runaway servant, ordered to serve 82 days.

Benjamin Hubbard v. Robert Latham. Judgt for Plf.

Page (325)

Susannah Klug appointed admr of her late husband George

Samuel Klugg; and Ambrose Powell, Benjamin Powell, Elliott Bohannon & Ephraim Rucker, appr's.

Will of John Hemingway proved by Thomas Baker.

James Kennerley appointed admr., & John Strother, William Covington, Henry Gambill & Thomas Baker apprs.

Page (326)

Will of James Wilder exhibited by his widow Peggy Wilder, proved by William Green, Robert Green & Robert Slaughter; and William Lightfoot, James Green & Joseph Norman appointed appraisers.

Deed James Wilder & Peggy, his wife, to William Green, proved by Robert Green.

Deed John Lillard & Susanna, his wife, to Thomas Lillard recorded.

Benjamin Johnston v. John Crawford. Cont'd on security of William Crawford.

Page (327)

John Lillard witness for James Ross v. William Meldrum, allowed 100 lbs. tobo. for 4 days.

Deed John Hammitt & Sarah, his wife, to John Forgeson recorded.

Petition of James Finnie to turn road objected to by William Kirtley, & continued.

James Shurley appointed road surveyor on motion of Christopher Crigler.

Robert Duncanson v. William Crawford. Judgt for Plf.

Page (328)

William Ball took oath as Captain of Company of foot under William Green county lieutenant.

Ann Powell & William Walker appointed admrs of John Powell, decd.; & William Twyman, Thomas Burbridge, Thomas Rucher & Nathan Underwood apptd apprs.

John Glassford (merchant of Glasgow) v. Edward Collinsworth. Judgt against dft & Moredock McKenzie surety.

Account of Elizabeth Clore's dower in slaves of her late husband Michael Clore recorded.

Page (329)

Dekar Thompson v. Raleigh Corbin. Cont'd on security of Raleigh Duncan.

Deed of apprenticeship between Ambrose Powell &c., for James Harrison, orphan of John Harrison, decd, to Jacob Medley. Recorded.

William Turner v. Joseph Gaines. Dismissed on intervention of John Williams.

Hannah Gaines, witness for John Williams, allowed 25 lbs. of tobo. for 1 day.

Mary Gaines, witness for John Williams, allowed 25 lbs. of tobo. for 1 day.

Alexander Woodroe & John Neilson v. William Walle. Judgt

Page (330)

for Plf., against dft. & Benjamin Roberts Jr. & Richard Davison, sureties.

Alexander Woodroe & John Neilson v. James Murphy. Judgt against Dft. & William Johnston Jr. security.

John Jett appointed road surveyor in place of Dickie Latham.

James Barbour Jr. appointed admr. for John Henderson, decd., and William Kirtley, William Walker, Thomas Buford & John Buford appointed appraisers.

Page (331)

Andrew Cockran & Co. v. James Story. Judgt against Dft. & surety, Francis Slaughter the younger.

Lennox & Scott v. William Nalle. Cont'd on answer of Benjamin Roberts, garnishee.

William Russell took oath as Captain of Company of foot under William Green county lieutenant.

Page (332)

Edward Turner appointed ———— in place of Joshua Browning.

20 May 1763.

Present: Nathaniel Pendleton, William Williams, William

Brown, Benjamin Roberts & William Kirtley. Gent.
Thomas Burk v. William Corbin. Cont'd.
John Shackleford v. John Hammitt. Cont'd.
William Meldrum v. Job Popham. Cont'd.
Benjamin Davis v. William Slaughter. Judgt for Plf.

Page (333)

The King v. Richard Yancey. Presentment Cont'd.

Matthew Hawkins v. James Hawkins. Judgt for Plf. on attachment of horse in possession of James Gaines Jr. & Daniel Dulaney.

Appraisement of Est. of James Pendleton, decd. Recd.

Thomas Slaughter v. William Morgan. Cont'd.
William Roberts v. John Strother. Execution ordered.

Page (334)

Abraham Blewbaker v. William Oneale. Judgt for Plf.
Charles Lewis v. George Rootes. Cont'd.
John Campbell v. Benjamin Hawkins. Cont'd.
Robert Duncanson v. William Eastham. Judgt for Plf.

Page (335)

Joseph James v. Ambrose Powell. Cont'd.
Benjamin Hoomes v. Christopher Hoomes. Cont'd.
David McCullock v. Robert Eastham. Cont'd.
James Bailey v. John Connor. Cont'd.
William Detherage v. James McDaniel. Cont'd.
Ambrose Coleman v. William Kirtley. Cont'd.
James Crawford v. Christian Bingerman. Cont'd.

Page (336)

William Pinkard v. Zachary Petty. Plea & Cont'd.
Thomas Langdon v. John Smith. Cont'd.
Isaac Smith v. John Carpenter. Cont'd.
William Underwood v. Samuel Reeds, Lott Hackley & James Brown. Cont'd.

Philemon Kavanaugh v. Charles Kavanaugh, James Pendleton & Henry Pendleton Exrs of James Pendleton, decd. Revived against exrs.

Page (337)

James & Martin Dewitt v. Beaumont Sutton. Dismissed.

Joseph Stevens v. William Lightfoot. Cont'd.

John Latham v. John Shackleford. Cont'd.

William Perfect v. Benjamin Hughes. Cont'd.

William Crawford Jr. v. Thomas Hopper. Dismissed agreed.

Charles Dick v. David Ross. Judgt for Plf.

John Yancey v. Jacob Kindrick & William Green. Cont'd.

Page (338)

Sarah & William Montgomery of London v. Thomas Rucker admr of William Pierce, decd. Dismissed agreed.

Thomas Grayson v. Richard Parks. Cont'd.

Valentine Seveire v. Daniel Boon. Cont'd.

William Bradley, assignee of Wallace assignee or Robert Detherage v. William Rumsey. Dismissed agreed.

Michael Thomas v. Christian Franks. Cont'd.

Lenox & Scott v. John Bernhysle. Cont'd.

Page (339)

Findley Morrison v. William Underwood & Eleanor, his wife, Exix of Thomas Stubblefield. Judgt for Plf.

Thomas Threlkeld v. Gabriel Jones. Cont'd.

Bennett Rose v. Zachary Taliaferro. Cont'd.

John Grayson v. William Grayson, James Stevens, John Wallis & George Wetherall. Cont'd.

Page (340)

John Grayson v. James Shackleford & Alice his wife. Cant'd.

Charles Linch v. Malcum McMurry. Cont'd for service on Benjamin Davis, garnishee.

James Ross v. John Dickerson. Judgt for Plf.

Peter Lehew v. William Rice. Cont'd.

Elliott Bohannon v. Philemon Kavanaugh. Process against Dft. as special bail for Alexander Englis.

Page (341)

Lenox & Scott v. Benjamin Davis. Cont'd.

William Gale v. William Field. Cont'd.

William Gale v. Richard Yancey. Cont'd.

Lenox & Scott v. Benjamin Hoomes. Contt'd.

Page (342)

Benjamin Davis v. George McNeale. Cont'd.

David Vawter v. Samuel Young. Cont'd.
Edward Bush V. Benjamin Davis. Dismissed.
John Barnes v. William Turner. Dismissed.
David Vawter v. Richard Stanton. Cont'd.
William Walker v. David Thompson. Process awarded.
Edward Bush v. John Connor. Cont'd.
William Russell v. Richard Doggett. Cont'd.
William Stringfellow v. John Yoeman. Cont'd.

Page (343)

Morias Hansbrough v. Henry Elly. Cont'd.
John Boots v. Robert Middletown & Francis Nalle. Cont'd on security of William Johnston Jr.
Alexander McKettrick & Co. v. John Dickerson. Dismissed because Dft. no inhabitant of County.
Abbott White v. William Nalle. Dismissed agreed.
Lewis Yancey v. William Davis. Dismissed agreed.

Page (344)

Lewis Wallis v. Oliver ———— & Garfield Brown. Judgt for Plf.

Nicholas Porter v. Ambrose Powell. Cont'd.
John Strother v. Henry Gambill. Dismissed agreed.
James Buchannon v. William Lightfoot. Cont'd.
James Buchannon v. Joseph Gaines. Cont'd.
Benjamin Pendleton v. Walter Shropshire. Judgt for Plf.

Page (345)

John & William Knox v. William Tutt. Cont'd.
George Row v. John Kelly. Cont'd.
Allan Raines v. Richard Thomas. Dismissed.
Birkett Davenport v. John Shropshire. Cont'd.

Page (346)

John Benger v. Richard Scales. Cont'd.

Francis Slaughter, the younger, v. John Latham. Judgement for the plaintiff.

Charles Dick v. Valentine Morgan. Judgt for Plf. on verdict of following jury: Lewis Yancey, John Latham, Ambrose Bohannon, William Gosney, Smith Johnston, Henry Threlkeld, Thomas Grayson, Ephraim Hubbard, John Sanders. John Williams, James Stewart & Charles Seale.

Page (347)

John Tackett v. Richard Price. Judegment for plaintiff on verdict of following jury: Charles Yancey, John Yancey Jr., Richard Ship, William Gaines, Edward Watkins, William Nash, Coleman Brown, John Bartley, William Wiseman, Oliver Towles, William Pinkard & Nathaniel Brown.

Thomas Stanton v. Richard Bryan. Judgt for Plf. on verdict of same jury last above listed.

Benjamin Hoomes v. Christopher Hoomes. Appealed.

Page (348)

James Stewart, witness for John Tackitt, allowed 125 lbs. of tobacco for 5 days attendance.

Thomas Wale, witness for John Tackitt, allowed 175 lbs. of tobo. for 7 days.

Joseph Gaines v. James Cummins. Cont'd.

21 May 1763.

Present: Nathaniel Pendleton, Daniel Brown, Henry Pendleton & James Slaughter. Gent.

John Waller v. William Frogg. Judge for Plf.

Page (349)

James Dillard v. John Sanders. Cont'd on security of William Williams.

John Gordon v. William Eastham. Judgt for Plf.

William Allison,, assignee of Benjamin Weeks, v. William Dulany. Cont'd.

George Frazier & Alexander Wright v. Daniel Mooring. Cont'd.

Page (350)

Andrew Cockran & Co. v. Benjamin & George Cornelius. Cont'd.

Ditto	v. Samuel Short. No inhabitant. Dis'd.
do	v. John Miller. Judgt for Plf.
do	v. Benjamin Gambill. Judgt for Plf.
do	v. William Crawford. Judgt for Plf.
do	v. Smith Johnston. Judgt for Plf.

Page (351)

do v. Benonie Twentyman, cont'd. on security of William Field.

Peter How v. Francis Hill. Cont'd on security of John Flint.

    ditto   v. James Howerton. Dismissed. No inhabitant.

    do   v. James Griffin. Process awarded.

    do   v. John Crittendon.   ditto.

    do   v. William Slaughter. Cont'd.

    do   v. Benjamin Morgan. Cont'd.

    do   v. David Thompson. Process awarded.

    do   v. Catherine Thompson.   ditto.

Page (352)

    do   v. Hugh Freeman   do

    do   v. Robert Cave. Dismissed. No inhabitant.

    do   v. Betty Nash. Dismissed agreed.

    do   v. John Waite. Cont'd. Thomas Jones, surety.

    do   v. Thomas Baker. do John Strother, do

    do   v. Thomas Breedlove. Dismissed. No inhabitant.

Page (353)

————James v. Archibald Gillison. Cont'd on security of Francis Slaughter & William Robinson.

Joseph James v. John Kelly. Process awarded.

    do   v. Walter Shropshire. Cont'd.

Alexander Woodroe & John Neilson v. Spencer Haynie. Dismissed;—no inhabitant.

    do   v. Thomas Covington. Cont'd.

    do   v. Richard Murphy. Judgt for Plf.

    do   v. Thomas Murphy. New process awarded.

Page (354)

    do   v. William Roberts. Arrested & Cont'd.

    do   v. Jacob Nalle. Dismissed agreed.

    do   v. Elizabeth Haynie exrx of Antho. Haynie. Continued.

Ephriam Clark v. William & James Turner. Judgt for Plf.

John Turner v. William Crawford. Judgt for Plf.

John Turner v. James Allan. Continued.

Page (355)

Dekar Thompson v. Thomas Davenport. Dismissed.

William Turner v. Thomas Oxford. Continued.

Aminadab Thurstout, lessee of William Turner & Margaret, his wife, v. Ferdinand Holdfast. Thomas Oxford substituted Dft. in place of Ferdinand Holdfast, appeared by John Lewis Atty. Cont'd.

Oliver Towles v. Robert Floyd. Process awarded.

William Knox v. William Tutt. Judgt against Dft. & Richard Tutt, garnishee.

Page (356)

William Green v. Frederick Lipham. Cont'd.
Elizabeth Willis & William Willis, Exrs of William Willis decd. Continued.

Marty Connell v. Ambrose Bohannon. Cont'd.
John Daniel Jacobi v. Lewis Davis Yancey. Cont'd.
Stephen Fisher v John Sims. Cont'd.
Alexander Woodroe & John Neilson v. William Crawford. Dismissed agreed.

Alexander Woodroe & John Neilson v. John Crawford. Cont'd on security of James Slaughter & Gabriel Amiss.
William Turner v. Adam Campbell. Dismissed agreed.

Page (357)

Raleigh Corbin v. Ephriam Hubbard. Cont'd on security of William Ball.

Richard Parks, assignee of William Tutt v. Martin & Thomas Baker. Cont'd on security of John Strother.

John McGannon v. Benonie Twentyman. Cont'd on security of Thomas Oxford.

William Robertson v. John Lear Jr. Dismissed agreed.
Nathaniel Pendleton v. John & Robert Floyds. Process awarded.

Page (358)

Nathaniel Pendleton v. John Nicholson. Cont'd on security of William Green.
Edmund Pendleton v. Benjamin Hoomes. Process awarded.
Adam Broyle v. Christopher Moyer. Cont'd.
James Barbour Jr. v. Frederick Lipham. Cont'd.
Ambrose Bohannon v. James Gaines. Cont'd.
Appraisement of Est. of Matthias Blankenbeker. Cont'd.
Appraisement of Est. of Christopher Reapman. Cont'd.

Anthony McKettrick & Co. v. Benjamin Davis. Cont'd.
Anthony Strother v. William Rumsey. Cont'd.

Page (359)

John Daniel Jacobi v. William Pritchett & Wm. Frogg. New process awarded.
John McAllister v. Charles McQueen. Judgt for Plf.

George Roberts & Catherine, his wife, v. William Russell. Cont'd.

Margaret Weatherall, Admr of John Weatherall, decd, v. Samuel Moore. Continued.
Benjamin Moore v. Francis Pryor. Cont'd.

Page (360)

David Johnson v. Adam Campbell. Dismissed agreed.
Ambrose Camp v. John Shackleford. Judgt for Plf.
Frazier & Wright v. John Kindrick. Process awarded.
Joseph Blackwell & Co. v. John & William Crawford. Con.
James Walker v. Lewis Booten. Cont'd.
Andrew Cockran & Co. v. Martin Baker. Cont'd on security of Thomas Baker.

Page (361)

Lettice Stanton by Adam Banks next friend v. Thomas Stanton. Cont'd.
Paul Yowell v. James Hunt. Dismissed agreed.
Lenox & Scott v. William Edwards. Dismissed.
Richard Lewis v. William Brown. Dismissed.
William Green v. Thomas Yates. Cont'd.
James Gaines Jr. v. William Brown. Cont'd.
Henry Brinker v. William Meldrum, Clerk. Cont'd.

Page (362)

John Barnes v. Richard Yancey. Cont'd.

James Penny assignee of John Pickett v. Jacob Walle & William Holloway. Cont'd with Henry Pendleton, security.
Lettice Stanton v. Thomas Stanton, her husband. Cont'd.

Jacob Walle & Nanny, his wife, v. Samuel Kersey & Eleanor, his wife. Cont'd.
John Shackleford v. James Hammitt. Cont'd.

John Strother, witness for John McAllister v. Charles Mc-

Queen, allowed 75 lbs. of tobo. for 3 days.
Thomas Underwood v. James Hammitt.   Cont'd.

Page (363)

David Hudson v. James Davis.   Judgt for Plf. on verdict
of following jury: Samuel Clayton, Oliver Towles, James Ross,
John Sanders, Birkett Davenport, Charles Yancey, William
Winn, John Tackitt, John Yeoman, Robert Sims, Benjamin
Hughes & Samuel Moore.

James Pendleton succeeded Henry Pendleton as road surveyor.

Philip Peyton v. Benjamin Davis.   Judgt for Plf. on verdict
of jury same as above listed.

Page (364)

Joseph James v. James Cummins.   Cont'd.
John Hoard v. Philemon Kavanaugh.   Cont'd.

The hands under John Reynolds, overseer, exempted from
certain work.

John Leavell Jr., witness for David Hudson v. James Davis,
allowed 75 lbs. of tobo. for 3 days.

16 June 1763.

Present: Daniel Brown, John Slaughter, William Eastham,
Henry Field Jr. & George Weatherall.   Gent.

Inventory Est. of Christian Reapman.   Rec'd.

Deed John Jones & Catherine his wife to James Shurley recorded.

Deed John Wilhoit & Margaret his wife to William Morris.
Recorded.

Page (365)

James Slaughter v. Hugh Freeman.   Judgt for Plf. against
Dft. & James Pendleton, garnishee.

Deed George Moyer Jr. to James Barbour Jr.   Rec'd.

Ann Davenport, over 14 years of age, chose her brother
Birkett Davenport as her guardian.

Frederick Zimmerman's ordinary license renewed.

Peter How v. Francis Hill.   Judgt against Dft. & securities
Robert Leavell & John Flint.

Page (366)

On petition of Henry Netherton for ancient road at Courtney Norman's plantation, William Eastham, William Russell, John Frogg & James Kennerley, app't'd viewers.

Petition of Theobald Fite to be levy free rejected.
Petition of William Robertson et als for ancient Rawling way & Church way granted.
Admr. acct of Est. of Leonard Ligler, recorded.

Cornelius Mitchell appointed surveyor of roads where Thomas Corbin was late surveyor.

Appraisement of Est. of John Henderson, decd, rec'd.
Inventory of Est. of Peter Clore, decd, rec'd.

Alexander Woodroe & John Neilson v. John Crawford. Dismissed agreed.

Deed Isaac Smith & Margaret his wife to William Crossthwait, rec'd.

Page (367)

Thomas Underwood v. James Hammitt. Judgt against George Stringfellow, garnishee.
John Shackleford v. James Hammitt. Cont'd.

Petition of George Moyer Jr. to have effects which his grand father George Moyer had laid in with his son Christopher Moyer for his support & maintenance delivered to him for that use is by the court rejected.

Alexander Woodroe & John Neilson v. Thomas Covington. Cont'd with James Graves security.

Adam Clore chose his mother Barbara Clore as his guardian & the court appointed her guardian also of her other children, viz: Solomon, Delilah, Elizabeth, Moses & Susanna, under 14 years of age.

Page (368)

Francis Pryor appointed constable instead of John Favour.
William Russell v. Richard Doggett. Judgt for Plf. on verdict of following jury: Benjamin Hoomes, John Latham, Francis Gaines, Lewis Yancey, John Cooper, William Stringfellow, Alexander McQueen, William Robertson, John Nalle Jr., Moses

Green, Harbin Moore & George Roberts.

Marty Connell v. Ambrose Bohannon.   Judgt for Plf.

John Wllis, witness for Marty Cannell v. Ambrose Bohannon, allowed 50 lbs. of tobo. for 2 days.

John Lear Jr. opposed petition of Wm. Robertson et als for Rawling way & Church way; ordered that Christopher Hoomes, John Green, John Read & George Parsons view a way from Robert Hoppers to road that leads to the church & report.

Page (369)

Motion of Adam Barlor that church wardens bind out Christian Nelson, orphan of Philip Nelson, decd, to said Barlor to be taught trade of tailor.

Benjamin Hoomes v. John Latham.   Judgt for Plf.

John Barnes v. Edward Ballenger Jr.   Judgt for Plf.

John Barnes v. Richard Yancey.   Dismissed agreed.

Will of John Hemingway & Margaret Crone proved by William Baker & Rec'd.

Ordered that church wardens bind out William Skelton son of John Skelton.

Anthony Head appointed road surveyor from Popham Run to Ashley's Ford.

Thomas Chelton appt'd road surveyor from Hazel River to F. T. in place of Timothy Lisk.

Page (370)

New Commission of the Peace directed to Thomas Slaughter, William Green, Ambrose Powell, Thomas Scott, Nathaniel Pendleton, Daniel Brown, Robert Green, William Williams, John Strother, William Brown, Joseph Wood, John Slaughter, James Barbour Jr., Henry Pendleton, Benjamin Roberts, William Kirtley, William Eastham, James Slaughter, Henry Field Jr. & George Wetherall, being read, Thomas Slaughter took the usual oath of justice of the peace & of the County court of chancery, all which oaths were administered to him by James Barbour Jr. & Henry Pendleton & then Thomas Slaughter administered oaths to Ambrose Powell, Nathaniel Pendleton, Robert Green, William Williams, John Slaughter, James Barbour Jr., Henry Pendleton, Benjamin Roberts & William Kirtley.

21 July 1763.

Present: Ambrose Powell, Robert Green, William Williams, & Benjamin Roberts.   Gent.

Elizabeth Davis appt'd admrx of her husband William Davis, decd.

Gabriel Jones, John Gray, William Pollard & Garfield Brown appointed appraisers of William Davis Est.

Deed Robert Freeman to Oliver Clerk proved by John Shackleford, Bennitt Rose & Peter Bowmer & rec'd.

Deed John Strother to James McDaniel. Rec'd.

Page (371)

Will of Adam Wilhoit exhibited by Adam Broyle & Nicholas Bryole Exrs., proved by John Wayland, William Eastham & Jacob Broyle witnesses, & recorded, & following appraisers appt'd: James Rucker, Ephriam Rucker, William Walker & Thomas Kirtley.

William Williams ordered to list tithables in room of James Slaughter.

William Brown ordered to list tithables in room of George Wetherall.

David Vawter v. Job Breeding. Dft. surrendered & so discharged sureties: David Jackson & Mary, his wife, & John Collins.

Deed George Moyer to John Wayland. Rec'd.

Ordered that Ambrose Powell, Thomas Scott, & Nathaniel Pendleton be recommended to Governor as fit persons for office of sheriff.

Page (372)

Nathaniel Pendleton v. George Stevens. Judgt for Plf. against George Kinnaird, garnishee, who admitted possession of Jackett & Breeches of the dft.

Andrew Cockran & Co. v. Walter Shropshire. Jud. for Plf. against dft. as surety for his overseer, William Jarvis.

Robert Duncanson v. Thomas Stanton. Judgt against Thomas Kirtley, garnishee.

Page (373)

Benjamin Johnston v. John Crawford. Judgt for Plf.
Benjamin Johnston v. Benjamin Hoomes. Judgt for Plf.
Child & Crap v. Martin Baker. Judgt for Plf.

Page (374)

Child & Crap v. Daniel Dulaney. Judgt for Plf.

Thomas Slaughter commissioned Colonel of Militia & Philip Barbour & Benjamin Cave commissioned Captains of foot.

Thomas Scott & William Brown took oath as justices of the peace & county court of chancery.

Dickie Latham, witness for Thomas Latham, at suit of Richard Lewis allowed 25 lbs. tobo. for 1 day.

Thomas Underwood, witness for same, allowed 67 lbs. tobo. for 1 day & 14 miles from Fauquire County.
Joseph Blackwell v. William Frogg. Judgt for Plf.

Page (375)

William Pickett witness for Joseph Blackwell allowed 85 lbs. tobo. for 1 day & 25 miles from Fauquire County.

Childs & Crap v. Moses Burbig. Dismissēd.

Robert Adams & Sarah his wife v. William Russell & James Hunter. Ordered that dower be assigned by Robert Slaughter, Thomas Slaughter, William Green & Nathaniel Pendleton.

John Humphreys appt'd road surveyor from Nick's Gallows to Scott's Bridge, & Henry Pendleton ordered to divide hands between him & Cornelius Mitchell, former overseer.

Bill of sale Walter Shropshire to Thomas Porter. Recd.

William Walker appt'd guardian of Joseph, John& William, orphans of John Henderson, decd.

Page (376)

22 July 1763.

Present: Ambrose Powell, William Brown, Benjamin Roberts & William Kirtley. Gent.
Thomas Burk v. William Corbin. Cont'd.
John Shackleford v. John Hammitt. Cont'd.
William Meldrum v. Job Popham. Deposition of Oliver Towles to be taken before he leaves Colony.

Charles Lewis v. George Rootes. Judgt for Plf. on verdict of the following jury: Benjamin Hughes, William White, Evan Thomas, Lewis Yancey, Richard Young, William Pinkard, Robert Jones, William Corbin, Henry Stringfellow, James Griffin, Ambrose Camp & John Sampson.

Page (377)

The King v. Richard Yancey. Presentment Cont'd.
John Campbell v. Benjamin Hawkins. Cont'd.
Lewis Yancey v. Philemon Kavanaugh. Cont'd.

Joseph James v. Ambrose Powell.   Dismissed agreed.
Benjamin Hoomes v. Christopher Hoomes.   Cont'd.
David McCullock v. Robert Eastham.   Cont'd.
James Bailey v. John Connor.   Cont'd.
William Detherage v. James McDaniel.   Cont'd.

Page (378)

James Crawford v. Christian Bingerman.   Judgt for Plf.
Thomas Grayson v. Richard Parks.   Cont'd.
Valentine Seveire v. Daniel Boon.   Cont'd.
Michael Thomas v. Christian Franks.   Cont'd.
Thomas Threlkeld v. Gabriel Jones.   Cont'd.
Bennitt Rose v. Zachary Taliaferro.   Cont'd.
John Grayson v. William Grayson, James Stevens, John Wallis, & George Wetherall.   Cont'd.

Page (379)

John Grayson v. James Shackleford & Alice his wife. Cont'd.

Elliott Bohannon v. Philemon Kavanaugh.   Judgt for Plf.
Lenox & Scott v. Benjamin Davis.   Trial by jury, viz:

Benjamin Hughes, William Robertson, Evan Thomas, Lewis Yancey, Richard Young, William Pinkard, Robert Jones, William Corbin, Henry Stringfellow, James Griffin, Ambrose Camp, & John Sampson.   Verdict for Plf. Reconsidered. Same verdict again returned, & set aside by court.

Page (380)

William Gale v. William Field.   Judgt for Plf. on verdict of jury, viz: Anthony Strother, Martin Hardin, Samuel Clayton Jr., William Stringfellow, James Gaines, James Duncanson, Birkett Davenport, Benjamin Hoomes, John Lillard, Daniel Brown, Edward Watkins & Ephraim Hubbard.
William Stringfellow v. John Yoeman.   Judgt for Plf. on verdict of jury above listed except Reuben Long substituted for William Stringfellow.

Page (381)

Morias Hansbrough v. Henry Elly.   Cont'd.
George Row v. John Kelly.   Cont'd.
Margaret Wetherall, admx of John Wetherall, decd, v. Samuel Moore.,Cont'd.
Joseph James v. James Cummins.   Cont'd.
John Hoard v. Philemon Kavanaugh.   Cont'd.
Dekar Thompson v. Raleigh Corbin.   Cont'd.

Page (382)

Frazier & Wright v. Richard Davison.   Cont'd.
Lenox & Scott v. William Nalle.   Cont'd.
Thomas Slaughter v. William Morgan.   Judgt for Plf.
Thomas Langdon v. John Smith.   Cont'd.
Isaac Smith v. John Carpenter.   Cont'd.

Page (383)

William Underwood v. Samuel Reeds, Lott Hackley & James Brown.   Cont'd.

Philemon Kavanaugh v. Charles Kavanaugh, Henry Pendleton & James Pendleton, Exrs of James Pendleton.   Cont'd.

James Stevens v. William Lightfoot.   Cont'd.

John Latham v. John Shackleford.   Continued for report of referees.

William Perfect v. Benjamin Hughes.   Contd.
Lenox & Scott v. John Bernhysle.   Cont'd.
Peter Lehew v. William Price.   Cont'd.
Richard Vernon v. Richard Winslow.   Cont'd.

Page (384)

William Gale v. Richard Yancey.   Cont'd.
Indictment against Daniel Brown dismissed.
Indictment against John Cleek & Catherine Omash heard & dismissed.
Thomas Slaughter, William Green & Benjamin Roberts ordered to view & report on bridge over Brooke's Run.
Lenox & Scott v. Benjamin Hoomes.   Cont'd.
David Vawter v. James Yancey.   Dismissed agreed.
David Vawter v. Richard Stanton.   Dismissed agreed.
William Walker v. David Thompson.   Dismissed agreed.
Benjamin Davis v. George McNeale.   Answer of William Robertson, garnishee, continued.

Page (385)

Edward Bush v. John Conner.   Cont'd.
Nicholas Porter v. Ambrose Powell.   Judgt for Plf.
James Buchannon v. Joseph Gaines.   Dismissed agreed.
Nathaniel Pendleton v. James Hawkins.   Garnishee John Campbell discharged on motion of Cutbert Bullitt atty for Isaac Christman claimant of attached effects.
Henry Stringfellow witness for William Stringfellow v. John Yeoman, allowed 50 lbs. tobo. for 2 days.
Lewis Yancey like witness allowed the same.

Page (386)

Daniel Brown & William Eastham took oath as justices of

the peace and county court of chancery.

Former order on petition of Henry Netherton for ancient way at Courtney Norman's plantation not being complied with, John Frogg, James Kennerley, John Roberts & Robert Detherage ordered to view & report.

David Vawter v. Job Breeding. Judgt for Plf.

Ann Strother appt's admx of her husband Benjamin Strother decd, & Goodrich Lightfoot, Richard Young, James Turner & John Rossen appt'd appraisers.

Deed John Strother & Mary his wife to Thomas Griffin. Recorded.

Page (387)

Raleigh Corbin v. Ephraim Hubbard. Cont'd with William Pinkard & William Gosney, securities.

John Simpson v. William Willis & Elizabeth Willis, Exrs of John Willis, decd. Cont'd.

23 July 1763.

Present: Robert Green, William Williams, Daniel Brown, Henry Pendleton & William Eastham. Gent.

Ambrose Coleman v. William Kirtley. Cont'd.
John & William Knox v. William Tutt. Dismissed.
William Gosney v. Beaumont Sutton. Cont'd.

Page (388)

John Benger v. Richard Seales. Cont'd.
James Dillard v. John Sanders. Cont'd.
William Allison, assignee of Benjamin Weeks v. William Dulaney. Cont'd with George Henry, surety.

John Goodman & Mary, his wife, v. Benjamin Hughes. Cont'd.

Andrew Cockran & Co. v. George & Benjamin Cornelius. Process awarded.

Andrew Cockran & Co. v. Benonie Twentyman. Judgt for Plf.

Page (389)

Andrew Cockran & Co., v. Martin Baker. Cont'd.
Peter How v. James Griffin. Dismissed agreed.
  do   v. John Crittendon. Judgt for Plf.
  do   v. William Slaughter. Judgt for Plf.

Page (390)

do · v. Catherine Thompson. Process awarded.
do v. Hugh Freeman. Process awarded.
do v. John Waite. Cont'd.
do v. Thomas Baker. Cont'd.
Joseph James v. Archibald Gillison. Process awarded.

Page (391)

do v. John Kelley. Cont'd.
do v. Walter Shropshire. Cont'd. ·
Alexander Woodroe & John Nielson v. Thomas Murphy. Judgt for Plf.
do v. William Roberts. Dismissed.
do v. Elizabeth Haynie exrx of Anthony Haynie, decd. Dismissed.
James Turner v. James Allan. Cont'd.

William Turner & Margaret, his wife, v. Thomas Oxford. Continued.
Oliver Towles v. Robert Floyd. Cont'd.

Page (392)

William Green v. Thomas Yates. Cont'd.
William Green v. Frederick Lipham. Cont'd.
John Daniel Jacobi v. Thomas Covington. Cont'd.
do. v. Lewis Davis Yancey. Cont'd.
Stephen Fisher v. John Sims. Dismissed agreed.
Richard Parks assignee of William Tutt v. Thomas & Martin Baker. Cont'd.

John McGannon v. Benonie Twentymen. Judgt for Plf.
Nathaniel Pendleton v. John & Robert Floyd. Process.
do. · v. John Nicholson. Judgt for Plf.

Page (393)

Edmund Pendleton v. Benjamin Hoomes. Cont'd.
Adam Broyle v. Christopher Moyer. Dismissed agreed.
James Barbour Jr. v. Frederick Lipham. Cont'd.
Ambrose Bohannon v. James Gaines Jr. Cont'd.
Appraisement Est. of Matthias Blankenbeker. Cont'd.

John Daniel Jacobi v. William Pritchett & William Frogg. Dismissed in part, & cont'd.

George Frazier & Alexander Wright v. Jacob Kindrick. Continued.

John Walker v. Lewis Booten. Cont'd.
Lettice Stanton by Adam Banks next friend v. Thomas Stanton. Cont'd.

Page (394)

James Gaines Jr. v. William Brown. Cont'd.
Jacob Nalle & Nanny his wife v. Samuel Kersey & Eleanor his wife. Cont'd.

George Frazier & Alexander Wright v. Daniel Mooring. Judgment for the Plaintiff.

Page (395)

Alexander Woodroe & John Nielson v. Thomas Covington. Continued.

Petition of John Lear Jr., for review of road. Cont'd.

Birket Davenport v. John Shropshire. Judgt for Plf. on verdict of jury, viz: John Dillard, James Duncanson, James Pendleton, Edward Watkins, Benjamin Hoomes, Ephraim Hubbard, Thomas Marshall, William Gosney, Martin Hardin, Lewis Yancey, William Pinkard & Zachary Petty.

Alexander McKettrick & Co. v. Benjamin Davis. Dismissed agreed.

Francis Strother v. William Rumsey. Cont'd.
Richard Lewis v. Thomas Covington. Cont'd.

Page (396)

John Boots v. Robert Middleton & Francis Walle. Cont'd.
Henry Brinker v. William Meldrum. Judgt for Plf. on verdict of jury, viz: names same as last above copied.
John Clore v. John Berry. Dismissed.
George Goggens v. Benjamin Rogers. Dismissed agreed.

Page (397)

William Pinkard v. Zachary Petty. Judgt on verdict of following jury: John Dillard, James Duncanson, James Pendleton, Edward Watkins, Benjamin Hoomes, William Gosney, Martin Harden, Lewis Yencey, Birket Davenport, Richard Young, John Marshall, & Benjamin Hughes.

George Goggans v. Peter Butler. Dismissed agreed.
John Harvey v. William Threlkeld. Judgt for Plf.
Charles Dick v. Thomas Latham. Judgt for Plf.
Dekar Thompson v. Alexander Laing. Cont'd.

Page (398)
do.   v. Robert Scott. Dft. arrested.

James Lesley v. Herman Husle & William Hansford. Process awarded.

Charles Stewart assignee of Frederick Lipham v. Jotn Hansford. Dismissed. Dft. no inhabitant of county.

William Johnston v. James Craigg, Clerk. Cont'd with Cuthbert Bullitt, surety.

James Gaines v. Francis Gaines. Cont'd.

Isaac Chrisman v. William Field. Cont'd.

Martin Hardin v. David Davis. Judgt for Plf.

Martin Hardin v. George Hume admr of George Hume decd. Continued.

Page (399)

Anthony McKettrick & Co. v. Simon Heninger. Cont'd. with Thomas Marshall surety.

    ditto   v: Neale McKully. Cont'd.

    do   v. Richard Watson. Process awarded.

    do   v. George Christall. Judgt for Plf.

    do   v. Thomas Hughes Jr. Judgt for Plf.

    do   v. James Murphy. Judgt for Plf.

Page (400)

Anthony McKettrick & Co. v. Benjamin Turner. Judgt for Plf.

    do.   v. Thomas Wright Sr. Judgt for Plf.

William Walle v. John Strother. Cont'd.

William Robinson v. John Frogg & John Clayton. Judgt for Plf.

Gilbert Morgan v. Richard Harmon. Cont'd.

Robert & James Duncanson v. Daniel Mooring. Dismissed.

    Ditto.   v. Richard Grymes. Cont'd with Nathaniel Pendleton, surety.

Page (401)

John Wright v. Daniel & William Dulaney. Jud. for Plf.

David Vawter v. Thomas Pierson. Cont'd.

David Vawter v. Thomas Jollet. Cont'd with William Batte surety.

William Robinson v. Charles Kavanaugh. Judgt for Plf.

Robert & James Duncanson v. Thomas Sampson. Process.

Nathaniel Pendleton v. Walter Shropshire. Cont'd.

Page (402)

On motion of William Williams surety for Richard Doggett Admr of his father, George Doggett, the Admr was ordered to give counter security.

Nathaniel Pendleton v. John Connor. Judgt for Plf.

David Davis v. Timothy Lisk & Jonas Jenkins Jr. Dft fined for not attending as witness against Martin Hardin.

John Branham v. Spencer Thadeus Branham. Judgt for Plf.

William Pinkard v. Thomas Marshall. Judgt for Plf.

Page (403)

Gabriel Amiss v. Thomas Aubury. Dismissed agreed.
John Sampson v. William Meldrum, Clerk. Dis'd agreed.
John Leavell v. Ambrose Camp. Cont'd.
John Sampson v. Humphrey Scroggin. Dis'd agreed.
Peter How v. Thomas Williams. Cont'd.
Neale McKully v. French Strother. Dismissed.
Child & Steel v. William Turner. Cont'd on security of Robert Duncan.
John Green v. Thomas Murphy. Judgt for Plf.

Page (404)

Edward Bush v. James Griffin. Cont'd.
Thomas Howell v. Abraham Cooper. Process awarded.
Betty Beverly v. Thomas Gibson. Cont'd.
Gabriel Jones v. John Shackleford. Cont'd.
John Williams v. John Grayson. Cont'd.
John & William Knox v. William Pinkard. Cont'd.

Page (405)

John Obannen, William Obannen & Jacob Hite Exrs of Bryan Obannen, decd. v. John Shackleford & James Slaughter. Process awarded.
Artomenus Robertson v. Michael Gowing. Dismissed.
William Johnston Jr. v. William Field. Dis'd agreed.
John Berry v. John Clore. Dismissed agreed.
Moses Green v. Philemon Kavanaugh. Dis'd agreed.
James Walker v. Benjamin Davis. Dismissed agreed.
Adam Broyle v. John Clore. Dismissed.
William Oneal v. George Moyer. Dismissed.
Thomas Ballard v. John Connor. Cont'd.
John Tilman v. Walter Shropshire. Cont'd.

John Lillard, witness for Martin Hardin v. David Davis allowed 75 lbs. tobo. for 3 days.

Page (406)

Richard Davis, witness for William Pinkard v. Zachary Petty, allowed 75 lbs. tobo. for 3 days.

Samuel Kersey, witness for William Pinkard v. Zachary Petty allowed 75 lbs. tobo. for 3 days.

18 August 1763.

Present: Thomas Slaughter, Ambrose Powell, Robert Green & Benjamin Roberts. Gent.
Edward Thomas v. Thomas Newman. Judgt for Plf.
Inventory of Est. of Benjamin Strother, Recorded.
Inventory Est. of James Wilder decd, recorded.
Malichiah Berry (constable) v. William Pendleton. Summons issued.
Deed William Tapp to Lewis Tapp his son, recorded.

Page (407)

Deed John Griffin & Frances his wife to Stephen Souther, recorded.

John Crittendon, guardian of Sarah Rogers, orphan of Joseph Rogers, decd, rendered account. Rec'd.

William Rogers, guardian of Joseph Rogers, orphan of Joseph Rogers, dec'd, rendered account.   Rec'd.

Will of Peter Weaver, decd, exhibited by John & Matthias Weaver Exors, proved by Michael Yeager & Michael Utz witnesses, recorded, & Benjamin Powell, William Sparks, Michael Russell & Adam Wayland apprs.

Artemenus Robertson v. Michael Gowing. Attachment reinstated.

James Bailey v. John Connor. Arritrators appointed, viz: Wharton Ransdell, Yelverton Peyton & Duff Green. Judgt for Plf.

William White, witness for James Bailey, allowed 230 lbs. tobo. for 3 days & 27 miles from Fauquire.

Page (408)

Ann Creal witness for John Connor v. James Bailey allowed 120 lbs. tobo. for 1 day & 32 miles from Fauq'r.

Elizabeth Bailey witness for same allowed same.

James Barbour Jr. v. William Oneal. Cont'd on security of Michael Oneal.

James Barbour Jr. v. Theobald Foite. Dismissed agreed.
Deed Benjamin Watts to John Watts proved by Joseph Wood & John Cave, & recd.

Tithe of William Turner added to list of Henry Field Jr.
2 tithables of Edward Lampkin added to list of Henry Field Jr.

David Hudson, guardian of Salmon's orphans ren'd acct.
Betty Nash, guardian of Nash's orphans, ren'd acc't.

Page (409)

Admr's acct of Susanna Cole, decd, recd.
William Dulaney's tithe added to list of William Williams.
Alexander Woodroe & John Nielson v. William Head. Dft. surrendered, and discharged William Field, surety.

Thomas Davis v. William Head. Dft. surrendered &c. same as above.

Samuel Orr v. Reuben Payne & John White. Cont'd with William Field, surety.

James Barbour Jr. v. John Flynt. Dismissed agreed.

William Field, Martin Nalle, & Joseph King exhibited commissions from the Governor appointing them lieutenants, & James Graves produced commission appointing him ensign of militia of the county under William Green, County Lieutenant, & they took usual oaths.

Page (410)

James Spilman, Joshua Browning, James Nash, lieutenants, Gabriel Amiss & Christopher Crigler, Ensigns severally produced commissions & took usual oaths.

Jeremiah Sims, witness for James Ross v. William Meldrum, Clerk, allowed 100 lbs. tobo. for 4 days.

William Green, Sheriff, objected to sufficiency of prison, ordered that Nathaniel Pendleton, Daniel Brown & William Williams let contract for repairs.

David Vawter v. Thomas Jollet. Judgt for Plf.

Anthony McKettrick & Co. v. Charles Seale. Judgt against Dft. & William Johnston, surety.

Page (411)

Gabriel Jones v. John Shackleford. Judgt for Plf.
Lewis Wallis v. Silas Hansford, John Harvey & Daniel Brown. Judgt against Dfts. and William Underwood & James

Hackley, sureties.

Lewis Wallis v. Moses Lindsey, Silas Hansford & Thomas Harper. Judgt against Dfts. & William Underwood & James Hackley, sureties.

Page (412)

Samuel Orr v. William Turner. Cont'd with George Roberts, surety.

David Vawter v. Thomas Maxwell. Judgt for Plf.

James Buchannon v. Joshua Browning. Dismissed agreed.

John Daniel Jacobi v. Thomas Covington. Judgt for Plf.

Page (413)

Ditto   v. Lewis Davis Yancey. Judgt for Plf.

William Johnston v. James Craig, Clerk. Dism'd agreed.

Timothy Lisk, witness for David Davis v. Martin Hardin, fined 350 lbs. tobo. for failure to attend.

Andrew Cockran & Co. v. Benjamin & George Cornelius. Cont'd with Adam Barlor, security.

Anthony McKettrick & Co. v. Lewis Washbourne. Judgt against Dft. & Richard Nalle, surety.

Page (414)

19 Aug. 1763.

Present: Thomas Slaughter, Ambrose Powell, William Williams & Benjamin Roberts. Gent.

Lenox & Scott v. William Nalle. Judgt against Dft. & Benjamin Roberts, garnishee.

Thomas Langdon v. John Smith. Cont'd.

Isaac Smith v. John Carpenter. Cont'd till tomorrow.

William Underwood v. Samuel Reeds, Lott Hackley & James Brown. Cont'd.

Page (415)

Philemon Kavanaugh v. Charles Kavanaugh, Henry & James Pendleton, Exrs of James Pendleton. Cont'd.

Joseph Stevens v. William Lightfoot. Cont'd.

John Latham v. John Shackleford. Continued for referees to make their final report.

William Perfect v. Benjamin Hughes. Cont'd.

John Glassford, assignee of Philip Riley, v. William Lewis. Cont'd.

Charles Linch v. William McMurry. Dismissed.

Peter Lehew v. William Rice. Dismissed.

Richard Vernon v. Richard Winslow. Dismissed.

Lenox & Scott v. Benjamin Hoomes. Cont'd.

Benjamin Davis v. George McNeale. Abated by death of Plf.

Edward Bush v. John Connor. Cont'd.

Raleigh Corbin v. Ephraim Hubbard. Cont'd.

Page (416)

John Sampson v. William Willis & Elizabeth Willis Exrs of John Willis, decd. Dismissed.

Alexander Waugh, witness for above Dfts. allowed 98 lbs. tobo. for 2 days & 16 miles from Orange County.

Alexander McDaniel & Isabella his wife, witnesses for above Plf. allowed 460 lbs. tobo. for 5 days & 16 miles from Orange County.

William Gosney v. Beaumont Sutton. Dismissed on answer of Joseph James, garnishee.

William Allison, assigne of Benj. Weeks, v. William Dulaney. Continued.

John Goodman & Mary, his wife, v. Benjamin Hughes. Dismissed agreed.

Robert Beverly v. Benjamin Hoomes. Cont'd on security of William Green & William Brown.

Page (417)

Peter How v. Catherine Thompson. Judgt for Plf.

Do. v. Hugh Freeman. Cont'd on security of Robert Freeman.

Joseph James v. John Kelly. Cont'd.

Do. v. Walter Shropshire. Judgt for Plf.

William Turner & Margaret, his wife, v. Thomas Oxford. Continued.

Page (418)

Oliver Towles v. Robert Floyd. Cont'd.

William Green & Co., v. Thomas Yates. Judgt for Plf.

Do. v. Frederick Lipham. Dismissed agreed.

Nathaniel Pendleton v. John & Robert Floyd. Judgt against defts. & Robert Hutcheson, surety.

Edmund Pendleton v. Benjamin Hoomes. Cont'd.

Anthony Strother v. William Rumsey. Cont'd.

Ambrose Bohannon v. James Gaines Jr. Cont'd.

Page (419)

John Daniel Jacobi v. William Pritchett. New process.

George Frazier & Alexander Wright v. Jacob Kindrick. Con.

Lettice Stanton v. Thomas Stanton. Cont'd.

Jacob Walle & Nanny his wife v. Samuel Kersey & Eleanor his wife. Cont'd.

John Boots v. Francis Walle. Plea of duress on dft. at house of William Priest in Culpeper County.

Page (420)

Richard Lewis v. Thomas Covington. Cont'd

Dekar Thompson v. Alexander Laing. Dismissed agreed.

Dekar Thompson v. Robert Scott. Cont'd on security of William Johnston.

James Lesley v. Herman Husle & William Hansford. Cont'd on security of John Clayton.

James Gaines Jr. v. Francis Gaines. Cont'd.

Page (421)

Isaac Chrisman v. William Field. Judgt for Plf.

Martin Hardin v. George Hume Admr of George Hume decd. Continued.

Anthony McKettrick & Co. v. Simon Heminger. Judgt against Dft. & Thomas Marshall, security.

Anthony McKettrick & Co. v. Neale McKully. Cont'd on security of John Latham.

Ditto. v. Richard Watson. Dismissed.

William Walle v. John Strother. Cont'd.

Gilbert Morgan v. Richard Herman. New process.

Page (422)

Robert & James Duncanson v. Richard Grymes. Cont'd.

David Vawter v. Thomas Pierson. Judgt against Dft. &

William Robinson, security.
Nathaniel Pendleton v. Walter Shropshire. Cont'd.
Tithe of Rice Bowen added to list of this year.
4 tithables of Richard Brooke added to list of this year.
John Leavell v. Ambrose Camp. Dismissed agreed.
Peter How v. Thomas Williams. New process.

Page (423)

Child & Steele v. William Turner. Judgt against Dft &
Robert Duncan, surety.
Edward Bush v. James Griffin. Cont'd.
Thomas Howell v. Abraham Cooper. Dismissed.
Betty Beverly v. Thomas Gibson. Cont'd.
James Williams v. John Grayson. Cont'd.
John & William Knox v. William Pinkard. Judgt for Plf.

Page (424)

John & William Obannen v. Jacob Hite, Exrs of Bryan O-
bannen v. John Shackleford & James Slaughter. Cont'd.

Thomas Ballard v. John Connor. Judgt against Dft. &
Nathaniel Pendleton, garnishee.
Nathaniel Pendleton v. Ephraim Hubbard. Judgt for Plf.
John Yancey v. Jacob Kendrick & William Green. Cont'd.

Page (425)

William Walle v. Robert Eastham. Cont'd.
John Clore v. Adam Broyle. Dismissed.
John Morgan witness for John Simpson v. Wm. & Eliz. Wil-
lis allowed 215 lbs. tobo. for 5 days & 10 miles from Orange
County.
John Robins witness as above allowed 107 lbs. tobo. for 2
days & 19 miles from Orange County.
Thomas Burk v. William Corbin. Cont'd.
John Shackleford v. John Hammitt. Cont'd.
William Meldrum v. Job Popham. Cont'd.
John Campbell v. Benjamin Hawkins. Cont'd.
Lewis Yancey v. Philemon Kavanaugh. Judgt for Plf.

Page (426)

Benjamin Hoomes v. Christopher Hoomes. Cont'd.
Daniel McCullock v. Robert Eastham. Cont'd.
John Tilman v. Walter Shropshire. Cont'd.
Benjamin Pendleton v. Walter Shropshire. Cont'd.

Benjamin Johnston v. Walter Shropshire. Cont'd.
Tithe of Murdock McKenzie added to list of John Slaughter.
Tithe of James Crow added to list of Joseph Wood.
Tithe of Hugh Sanders added to list of Nathaniel Pendleton.
William Detherage v. James McDaniel. Verdict for Dft. by
the following jury; Edward Watkins, Joseph James, Dickie
Latham, Samuel Clayton Jr., John Shackleford, Ambrose
Camp, French Strother, John Clayton, William Robertson,
John Yancey Jr., Richard Pollard & Anthony Foster.

Page (427)

Ambrose Coleman v. William Kirtley. Dismissed.
John White, witness for James McDaniel v. William Deth-
erage, allowed 100 lbs. tobo. for 4 days.
Abraham Cooper, like witness, same allowance.
John Cock, same as last above.
Bennitt Rose v. Zachary Taliaferro. Cont'd.

Page (428)

20 August 1763.

Present: Ambrose Powell, Daniel Brown, William Williams,
and John Slaughter. Gent.

Alexander Woodroe & John Nielson v. William Head. Cont'd.
Thomas Davis v. William Head. Cont'd.
Anthony McKettrick & Co. v. John Crawford. Cont'd on
security of Christopher Hoomes.
     Ditto.   v. Ephraim Hubbard. New process.

Page (429)

     do   v. Richard Watson & Richard Nalle.

James Barbour Jr. v. Adam Barlor. Cont'd on security of
Robert Applebee.
     Ditto   v. John Kelly. Judgt for Plf.
     do   v. John Rush. Judgt for Plf.
     do.   v. William Hensley. Judgt for Plf.
     do.   v. James Henson. Judgt for Plf.
     Ambrose Bohannon v. John Wallis. Cont'd.

Page (430)

     Ditto.   v. Abbott ————. Dismissed agreed.
     do.   v. Francis Strother. Cont'd.
     do.   v. Gabriel Loving. Judgt for Plf.

do.   v. Lawrence Bradley.   Judgt for Plf.
do.   v. John Gambell.   Judgt for Plf.
do.   v. Martin Baker.   Judgt for Plf.
do.   v. William Baker.   Judgt for Plf.

Page (431)

do.   v. Martin Davenport.   Dismissed agreed.
William Akin v. Elizabeth Croney.   Abated by death of Dft.
   ditto.   v. James Kennerley admr of John Hemingway,
decd.   Judgt for Plf.
Moses Bledsoe v. Frederick Zimmerman.   Cont'd.
John Pendleton & Co. v. Zachary Cogwell.   Judgt for Plf.
   do.   v. William Moore.   Judgt for Plf.
Benjamin Johnston v. Elizabeth Blanton.   New process.

Page (432)

David Vawter v. Ursulla Knight.   Process awarded.
James Gildart, Merchant of Liverpool v. James Hackley.
Dismissed.
James Gildart, merchant in Liverpool, v. William Strother.
Dismissed.   Dft. no inhabitant of Co.
   Ditto   v. Anthony Goleson.   Ditto.
William Hedgeman v. Reuben Payne.   Cont'd.
Dekar Thompson v. George Stringfellow.   Judgt for Plf.
James Glandenning v. William Slaughter.   Judgt for Plf.
Peter How v. Henry Jones.   Cont'd.

Page (433)

Joseph Jones v. Thomas Burk.   Dismissed.
   ditto.   v. Richard Vawter.   New process awarded.
   do.   v. Richard Breedingcross.   Judgt for Plf.
   do.   v. Benjamin Hoomes.   Judgt for Plf.
Hugh Freeman v. William Slaughter.   Cont'd with John
Johnston, surety.
Valentine Seveire v. Daniel Boon.   Cont'd.
Michael Thomas v. Christian Franks.   Cont'd.
Thomas Threlkeld v. Gabriel Jones.   Dismissed.
Robert Adams v. William Russell & James Hunter.   Cont'd.
Petition of Henry Netherton et als to establish old way of
road to Courtney Norman's plantation.   Cont'd.

Page (434)

John Grayson v. James Shackleford.   Dismissed.
Morias Hansborough v. Henry Elly.   Cont'd.

George Row v. John Kelly. Cont'd.

John Hoard v. Philemon Kavanaugh. Judgt for Plf.

Margaret Ham, witness for John Hoard against Philemon Kavanaugh, allowed 125 lbs. tobo. for 5 days.

Thomas Grayson v. Richard Parks. Judgt for Plf. on verdict of jury, viz: Alexander Mchurd, Neal McCawley, Frederick Zimmerman, William Gaines, James Lillard, Benjamin Hoomes, Thomas Oxford, William Hutcheson, John Hoard, Ambrose Bohannon, James Graves & John Duncan.

Page (435)

George Morton v. William Harper. Cont'd with Philemon Kavanaugh, surety.

James Coursey v. Offill. Cont'd.

Robert & James Duncanson v. Francis Strother. Dis'd.

John Hastie v. William Pound. Cont'd.

John Spotswood, infant, by Bernard Moore, next friend v. William Moore & Zachary Cogwell. Cont'd.

Page (436)

John Leavell v. James ——inor. Judgt for Plf.

Ditto.   v. William Slaughter. New process.

do.   v. Robert Applebee. Judgt for Plf.

Joseph James v. James Cummins. Judgt for Plf. on verdict of jury, viz: Alexander Mchurd, Neal McCawley, Frederick Zimmerman, William Gaines, James Lillard, Benjamin Hoomes, Thomas Oxford, William Hutcheson, Nicholas Green, Ambrose Bohannon, James Graves & John Duncan.

Philemon Kavanaugh, guardian of Ann Kavanaugh infant rendered his account.

Frazier & Wright v. Richard Davison. Cont'd.

Page (437)

James Dillard v. John Sanders. Judgt for Plf.

Andrew Cockran & Co. v. Benonie Twentyman. Judgt for Plf. on verdict of jury above named.

Page (438)

Andrew Cockran & Co. v. Martin Baker. Judgt for Plf, on verdict of jury last above listed.

Page (439)

Isaac Smith v. John Carpenter. Dismissed.

Peter How v. Thomas Baker. Judgt for Plf., on verdict of same jury last above listed.

William Turner & Margaret his wife v. Thomas Oxford. Continued.

John Moore v. Robert Coleman & Nicholas Green. Cont'd.

Page (440)

Alexander Woodroe & John Nielson v. Reuben Crawford. Dismissed—Dft. no inhabitant of county.

William Thomas & Francis Kirtley, Exrs, of Francis Kirtley, decd v. Benjamin Powell. New process.

James Slaughter v. Ephraim Hubbard. Cont'd with Martin Dewitt, surety.

John Laysons v. Anthony Garnett. New process.
Gabriel Jones Jr. v. Joseph Amiss. Cont'd.
Martin Pickett v. William Bragg. Dismissed. Dft. no inhabitant of county.

Page (441)

Thomas Wright Jr. v. William Field. Cont'd with Thomas Oxford surety.
William Allison v. Valentine Morgan. Cont'd.
French Strother v. John Connor. Cont'd.
Christopher Crigler v. George Mullis & John James. Cont'd.
Marion Barnett v. William Cave. Dismissed.
Cuthbert Bullitt v. Walter Shropshire. Cont'd.
Artemenas Robertson v. Michael Gowing. Judgt for Plf.

Page (442)

French Strother commissioned lieutenant, & Reuben Long, Thomas Grayson & Thomas Oxford, ensigns, of militia under William Green county lieutenant severally took the usual oaths.

John Leavell v. Nicholas Green. Submitted to aubitrators: George Holt & Matthias Hawkins.
Nathaniel Pendleton v. John Nicholson. Dis'd Agreed.

1 September 1763.

Present: Thomas Slaughter, Nathaniel Pendleton, Daniel Brown & William Williams, Gent.

Andrew Lightly in custody of William Green sheriff charged with felony in stealing property of Hugh Freeman, convicted of misdemeanor & given 15 lashes on his bare back well laid on.

Page (443)

15 Sept. 1763.

Tithe of Robert Freeman added to list of William Williams.
Deed James Sims to his son John Sims. Recorded.
Inventory of Est. of Peter Weaver, recorded.
Negro boy of James Crow adjudged 14 years of age.
John Freeman v. George Hume. Dismissed agreed.
Deed Thomas Parsons to Samuel Fergeson. Recorded.
James Kennerley Adrm of John Hemingway decd v. William Baker. Cont'd with Thomas Davenport surety.

Page (444)

Benjamin Johnston v. Wyatt Coleman. New process.
William Johnston, Doctor, v. Brooke Jones. Cont'd.
Doctor William Johnston v. William Pitcher. Jud. for Plf.
Peter Oneal, infant by Michael Oneal, next friend, v. Michael Leatherer. Cont'd.
Robert & James Duncanson v. Joshua Lampton. Judgt for Plaintiff.

Page (445)

John Marshall v. David Vawter. Process awarded.
Dekar Thompson v. Lynn Banks. Judgt for Plf.
Appraisement Est. of William Davis, decd. Recorded.
William Allison v. William Field. Cont'd with Reuben Payne security.
Doctor John Sutherland v. John Bond. Dismissed.
  ditto. v. Thomas Doggett. Judgt for Plf.
  do. v. John Gray. Judgt for Plf.

Page (446)

James Hackley v. William Field. Cont'd with Thomas Oxford, surety.

Lenox & Scott v. John Cubbage. Dismissed agreed.

James Barbour Jr. v. Oliver Towles. Cont'd with Adam Barlor surety.

Frederick Zimmerman v. Thomas Griffin. Cont'd with Joseph James surety.

Dekar Thompson v. James Green. Cont'd.

Page (447)

Adam Barlor v. Francis Hill.   Judgt for Plf.

John Graham, witness for John Richardson v. William Corbin, allowed 345 lbs. tobo. for 3 days and 45 miles to and from Frederick County.

Anthony McKettrick & Co. v. John Cave.   Cont'd with William Field surety.

Henry Field Jr. qualified as vestryman of St. Marks' Parish.

Ambrose Barbour, John Latham, & Joseph Stewart commissioned lieutenants, Joseph Rogers, Thomas Sims & Adam Wayland, ensigns, took the several oaths.

John Berry appointed constable in place of Malachy Berry.

Page (448)

2 tithables of Robert Sanders added to Nathaniel Pendleton's list.

2 tithables of Nathaniel Sanders added to William Williams' list.

On motion of John Carpenter Jr., Nicholas Yeager, Nicholas Smith, Matthias Smith, Christopher Barlor& Jacob Barlor were added to road gang under John Yeager, overseer.

Agreement of Elizabeth Clore & John Clore Exor of Michael Clore decd, recorded.

Deed Fielding Lewis Atty for James Compton of Great Brittain to Michael Lawler, recorded.

George Morton v. William Harper.   Cont'd on surrender of Dft. by Philemon Kavanaugh, special bail.

William Allison v. John Grimsley.   Judgt for Plf.

Page (449)

Ditto.   v. Jeremiah Corbin.   Judgt for Plf.

David Vawter v. Ursulla Knight.   Cont'd.

William Akin v. James Kennerley Admr of Elizabeth Croney decd.   Cont'd.

William Green v. James Williams.   Cont'd.

Bernard Platt v. William Lightfoot.   Cont'd.

James Kennerley Admr of John Hemingway v. Rice Bowen. Cont'd with William Johnston surety.

Malachy Berry v. William Oneal.   Dismissed agreed.

Page (450)

Deed Thomas Stanton Jr. to David Vawter, proved by William Vawter, & recd.

John Alexander v. Julius Hunt.   Process awarded.

Order set aside which bound Christian Nelson, orphan to Adam Barlor; & wardens ordered to bind said orphan to Capt. Philip Barbour.

Wardens ordered to bind out Adam Nelson, orphan, to James Barbour Jr.

Isaac Chrisman v. John Campbell.   Cont'd. on security of Joseph Campbell.

Page (451)

Henry Field Jr. v. Henry Curtis.   Dismissed agreed.

Thomas Baker v. James Kennerley Admr of John Hemingway decd, submitted to John Lewis & Cuthbert Bullitt arbitrators.

William Pound v. William Watts.   Judgt for Plf.

Ambrose Bohannon v. William Frogg.   Judgt for Plf.

Francis Strother v. John Gambill.   Cont'd.

French Strother v. Samuel Moore.   Dismissed agreed.

John Pollard v. Humphrey Scroggin.   Dismissed agreed.

Page (452)

Michael Sloan v. James Freeman.   Dismissed.

John Slaughter & James Rucker, church wardens of Brumfield Parish, v. Elizabeth Kelly.   Dismissed agreed.

John Crawford v. Christopher Hoomes.   Cont'd.

William Field v. John Barnes.   Cont'd.

James Gildart, merchant of Liverpool v. James Hackley. Cont'd on security of Samuel Reeds.

Ditto.   v. Elliott Bohannon.   Cont'd on security of Joseph Jones.

Page (453)

Henry Souther v. Thomas Stanton.   Dismissed.

20 October 1763.

Present: Robert Green, Henry Pendleton, William Kirtley, & Henry Field Jr.   Gent.

10 tithables of William Lightfoot added to list of Henry Field.

Betty Nash guardian of orphans of William Nash decd rendered account.

Ambrose Powell, appointed sheriff, took usual oaths.

Sheriff Ambrose Powell appointed John Green, George Wetherall & William Johnston, under sheriffs, & they took the usual oaths.

Page (454)

John Roane assignee of John Cassell v. James Stewart Jr. Judgt against Dft. & his brother Charles Stewart, surety.

John Strother took oath as justice &c.

Daniel Philips petitioned for leave to erect mill across Robinson River opposite property of Robert Terrill, & sheriff ordered to select 12 freeholders to view & report.

Page (455)

3 deeds from William, Thomas & Francis Kirtley exrs of Francis Kirtley decd to Benjamin Roberts, recorded.

Same grantors to Timothy Acuff, recorded.

ditty to William Kirtley, recorded.

Deed James Wheatley to John Hume, recorded.

Deed Thomas Stanton to Elliott Bohannon Jr., proved by Henry Lewis, & Recd.

Deed Francis Lucas & Elizabeth his wife to John Amburger recorded.

Richard Hackley orphan of Joseph Hackley decd, chose James Hackley as his guardian.

Anthony McKettrick & Co. v. William Dulaney & Walter Butler. Cont'd on security of William Smith & James Butler.

Page (456)

Will of Thomas Rucker, decd, exhibited by Peter & John Rucker Exors, proved by Thomas Stanton Jr. & William Jackson Jr. witnesses, & William Walker, William Twyman, Nathaniel Underwood & Thomas Burbridge, app'td Aprs.

Will of John Medley decd exhibited by Jacob Ward & Elizabeth Medley Exors, proved by Zachary Gibbs & John Cave, witnesses, & Richard Vernon, Zachary Gibbs, John Burford & William Pendleton appointed oppraisers.

Page (457)

William Green late sheriff delivered up to Ambrose Powell, present sheriff the following persons now in the custody of the Goal, viz:

William Frogg for debts due John Waller & Ambrose Bohannon.

James Murphy for debts due Woodroe & Nielson.
Martin Baker for debt due Andrew Cockran & Co., & Child & Crop.

Thomas Baker for debts due Peter How.
Robert Applebee for debts due John Leavell.
William Walle for debts due Woodroe & Nielson.
Philemon Kavanaugh for debts due Andrew Cockran & Co. & George McCall.
Thomas Murphey for debt due Woodroe & Nielson.

Page (458)

Sam, negro boy of Frances Browning adjudged 10 yrs. old.
Janey negro girl of Frances Browning adjudged 12 yrs. old.

Hannah negro girl of Thomas Pratt adjudged 13 yrs. old.
Bess negro girl of William Sherrall adjudged 12 yrs. old.
Judy negro girl of Francis Slaughter Jr. adjudged 13 yrs. old.
Sam negro boy of Henry Stringfellow adjudged 8 yrs. old.

James Kennerley Admr of John Hemingway v. Rice Bowen. Cont'd on security of Murty Connell & Ephraim Clerk.
William Brown v. Isaac Chrisman.   Bill filed.
Deed of apprenticeship between Francis Hackley & George Stubblefield orphan.   Rec'd.

Deed of apprenticeship between Frank Hackley & Richard Hackley, orphan, recorded.

Page (459)

James Barbour Jr. v. Oliver Towles.   Dft. gave Daniel Goggens security instead of Adam Barlor.

Benjamin Smith v. Enoch Hill.   Judgt for Plf.
Oliver Towles v. Robert Floyd.   Dismissed agreed.
Ordered that William Green, Nathaniel Pendleton, Daniel Brown & William Williams let the building of a prison for this county.

15 Dec. 1763.

Present: Thomas Scott, Nathaniel Pendleton, William Williams, Joseph Wood, Benjamin Roberts, & Henry Field Jr. Gent.

Page (460)

Deed Henry Field & Esther his wife to William Sims. Recd.
Henry Field appointed admr of William Stanton, decd, & Di-

anah, his widow, relinquished her dower, & William Kirtley, Thomas Kirtley, Jeremiah Early & James Rucker Appointed appraisers.

Deed from Charles Oneal & Esther his wife, to James Riddle their son in law ackgd & recd.

Inventory Est. of John Powell, recorded.

Inventory Est. of Thomas Rucker, recorded.

William Porteas, servant of Edward Tinsley Jr., Complained of inhuman treatment, ordered that Tinsley pay the servant 50 shillings & costs, & discharged the servant from his indenture.

Page (461)

Deed Thomas Stanton to Elliott Bohannon, recd.

John Smith, witness for William Porteas, allowed 25 lbs. tobo. for 1 day.

John Graves, witness for same, allowed same.

Anthony McKettrick & Co. v. Neale McKully. Dft. surrendered by John Latham, special bail. Judgt for Plf.

Deed from Jacob Blankenbeker & Mary Barbara his wife to Jacob Medley, recorded.

On motion of George William Fairfax, 2596 acres of land added to list taken this year, & 4250 acres belonging to Miss Hannah Fairfax, added to same list.

Page (462)

Robert Cave, witness for William Porteas, allowed 25 lbs. tobo. for 1 day.

Ambrose Powell, sheriff, reported prison insufficient.

Robert Green renewed licence to keep ordinary.

The court proceeded to lay the levy	lbs. Tobacco
To Mr. Secretary Nelson by account	294
To John Lewis Gent. prospector for the king	2000
To Ambrose Powell, Sheriff, his salery	1248
To Roger Dixon, Clerk, his salery	1248
To ditto. by account	960
To John Spostwood Est. keeping Germ'a ferry	3000
To John Green sub sheriff	840
To Robert Coleman, Geoler by account	2070
To Robert Leavell for setting up post of direction	50
To John Carder, constable, & account	382
To Richard Price, constable, & acct	461
To Ditto for county levy overpaid last year	6

To John Barbee, constable, & account   261
To Malachy Berry, Constable, & account   700
To William White, Constable, & account   372
To William Johnston, sub sheriff, acct & delingts   126
To William Baker for a wolf's head & certificate   100
To John Duncan for 6 young wolves heads & certificate   300
To N. Pendleton Gent & acct for chairs for county   432
To John Thomas for post of Direction & Acct   50
To Ambrose Camp, & acct   2250
To Smith Johnston, Pattroller   80
To John Cole   Do   30
To Christopher Kabler Do   80
To Thomas Bryant   Do   30
To pay Ambrose Camp £5 for service done the county & to Poy Peter Taliaferro for building a bridge over Brookes Run to be sold by the sheriff & to account with the court for the overplus.   3500

    20870
To 6 &c. for collecting   1253
To a depositum in the sheriff's hands   2602

    24725

Cr. By a depositum in sheriff's hands last year   2948
By 3111 Tithes at 7£ nett Tobo & Poll   21777

Page (463)

    24725

Alexander Hawkins appointed constable in place of Richard Price.

William Johnston v. William Field. Judgt for Plf.

George Wetherall qualified as vestryman of Brumfield Parish in room of John Towles.

Ambrose Powell, sheriff, ordered to collect from Robert Eastham & James Slaughter, money in their hands belonging to the county.

Frances Browning petitioned for Rolling Road through land of John Cooper, and viewers appointed as follows: William Johnston Jr., William Duncan, John Roberts & Reuben Slaughter.

Page (464)

Nathaniel Pendleton ordered to acquaint Bernard Moore

Exor of John Spotswood, decd, that unless better attention is given to transportation of tobacco at Germanna Ferry the salery will be withdrawn, &c.

6 January 1764.

Present: Thomas Slaughter, Daniel Brown, Robert Green, & Henry Pendleton. Gent.

The following claims were certified to the General Assembly:

Robert Green, for taking up a runaway negro named Jamey belonging to Landon Carter Jr.

Frances Browning for flour for use of melitia.

William Roberts for bacon for use of melitia.

A claim of John Corbin for beef, indian meal, & a sack bag for the use of the melitia &c.

John Corbin, for 40 Diets for the melitia.

    do.   for 50 Diets for the melitia.

    do.   for 6 Diets for the melitia.

    do.   for 10 Diets for the melitia.

19 January 1764.

Present: Nathaniel Pendleton, Daniel Brown, William Williams & William Brown. Gent.

Deed Paul Plankenpeker & Margaret his wife to Adam Fisher. Recorded.

Page (466)

Deed George Rootes to Christopher Crigler, proved by Richard Young, Henry Lewis Jr. & William Chapman.

Deed George Rootes to William Chapman, proved by Richard Young, Henry Lewis Jr. & Stephen Fisher.

Toney & Toby, negro men of Charles Carter Jr., charged with hog stealing, found not guilty.

Janie, negro girl of Thomas Carington adj'd 9 yrs. old.

Gabriel Amiss appt'd constable in place of John Barbee.

Alexander Hawkins appt'd constable in place of Richard Price.

William Gambill, appointed constable.

Page (467)

Appraisement Est. of William Stanton, decd, recd.

Deeds Peter Fleshman to his sons Robert & Peter Fleshman, recorded.

Deed Ambrose Barnett to Francis Gibbs, recorded.

Deed Ambrose Barnett to John Beale. Rec'd.

On motion of James Slaughter for road near school house by Archibald Gillison's to his mill, Christopher Hutchins, John Barbee, James Spilman & Archibald Gillison appointed viewers.

On motion of Henry Field for road from Thornton's road a little below Madam Thornton's Quarter to the north branch of Hazel River commonly called the Great Wilderness, Timothy Lisk, James White, John Grayson & Richard Gaines appointed viewers.

Motion of Frances Browning for a Rolling Road from her plantation through land of John Cooper, Cont'd.

Nathaniel Pendleton v. Lewis Crain. Judgt for Plf.

Page (468)

William Brown v. William Wiseman. Judgt for Plf.

8 February 1764.

His Majesty's commission dated 13 January last past directed to Thomas Slaughter, William Green, Thomas Scott, Nahtaniel Pendleton, Daniel Brown, Robert Green, William Williams, John Strother, William Brown, Joseph Wood, John Slaughter, James Barbour Jr., Henry Pendleton, Benjamin Roberts, William Kirtley, William Eastham, James Slaughter, Henry Field Jr. & George Wetherall, or any four of them, &c.,

Pages (469 & 470)

by virtue of which Robert Green, William Williams, William Green & James Slaughter, Gent. named in the commission took the oaths &c.

Page (471)

Sheriff ordered to pay Roger Dixon, Clerk, for 4 record books out of money due county from Robert Eastham & James Slaughter.

Elliott Bohannon appointed vestryman of Brumfield Parish in place of Francis Kirtley, decd.

Gabriel Amiss appointed constable in place of John Barbee, took the usual oaths.

David Davis & John Berry, constables, took oaths, &c.

Deed George Rootes to Michael Crigler, proved by James Barbee Jr. & John Taylor Jr. Recd.

Deed George Rootes to James Barbour Jr. proved by Elliott

Bohannon, Ambrose Bohannon & William Brown.   Recd.
Lease John Shotwell to Allan Rains.   Recd.
Honorius & Ambrose Powell, orphans of John Powell, decd, chose James Powell, their brother, guardian.

Page (472)

Benjamin Johnston v. Wiatt Coleman.   Judgt for Plf.

On motion of James Barbour Jr. to turn road through old field of Adam Gaar to his Rolling Road, James Rucker, Ephrain Rucker, Elliott Bohannon & William Walker apponted viewers.

Report on motion of James Slaughter for road out of road that leads from Freeman's to Grinnal's Ford near school house by Gillison's to his mill returned, & ordered that John Jett & Frederick Fishback, with their gang of hands, clear the same. Adjourned.

NOTE.   Although a name may appear several times on a page, it is indexed only once. The paging called for is that of the original minute book indicated throughout in the foregoing abstracts.

INDEX

372.

KIRTLEY, Francis, 275, 309, 318, 440, 455, 471; James, 275; Margaret, 275; Thomas, 275, 371, 372, 460; William, 275, 311, 316, 327, 330, 332, 335, 370, 376, 387, 427, 453, 455, 460, 468.

KITE, Jacob, 424.

KLUGG, George Samuel, 325, Samuel, 273; Susannah, 325.

KNIGHT, Ursulla, 432, 449.

KNOX, John, 296, 302, 345, 387, 404, 423; William, 296, 302, 345, 355, 387, 404, 423.

LAING, Alexander, 397, 420.

LAMPKIN, Edward, 408.

LAMPTON, Joshua, 444.

LANGDON, Thomas, 280, 336, 282, 414.

LATHAM, Dickie, 274, 330, 374, 426; John, 281, 285, 292, 299, 301, 323, 324, 337, 346, 368, 369, 383, 415, 447, 461; Thomas, 374, 397.

LAWLER, John, 272; Michael, 448.

LAYSONS, John, 440.

LEAR, John, 323, 357, 368, 395.

LEAVELL, John, 296, 364, 403, 422, 436, 457, 442; Robert, 365, 462.

LEATHERER, Michael, 273, 305, 444.

LEHEW, Peter, 294, 340, 383, 415.

LENOX & SCOTT, 290, 297, 284, 285, 315, 331, 338, 361, 379, 382, 383, 384, 414, 415, 446.

LEWIS, Charles, 280, 334, 376; Fielding, 448; Henry, 455, 466; John, 309, 355, 451, 462; Richard, 315, 361, 395, 420; William, 415.

LESLEY, James, 398, 420.

LIGHTFOOT, Goodrich, 386; William, 281, 292, 301, 326, 337, 344, 383, 415, 453, 449.

LIGHTLY, Andrew, 442.

LIGLER, Leonard, 366.

LILLARD, James, 434, 436; John, 326, 327, 380, 397, 405; Susanna, 326; Thomas, 326.

LINCH, Charles, 279, 287, 340, 415.

LINDSEY, John, 315; Moses, 411.

LIPHAM, Frederick, 356, 358, 392, 393, 398, 418; Jacob, 302.

LISK, Timothy, 369, 402, 413, 467.

LONG, Reuben, 275, 288, 319, 380, 442.

LOVE, William, 294.

LOVING, Gabriel, 430.

LUCAS, Elizabeth, 455; Francis, 455.

LYRLE, Christopher, 307.

MANIFEE, John, 323; Jonas, 323.

MARSHALL, John, 397, 445; Thomas, 395, 396, 399, 402, 421.

MARTIN, Mary, 324.

MAXWELL, Thomas, 412.

MAYFIELD, John, 318.

MCALLISTER, John, 311, 359, 362.

MCCALL, George, 457.

MCCAWLEY (McKully), Neale, 301, 434, 436.

MCCULLOCK, Daniel, 426; David, 335, 377.

MCDANIEL, Alexander, 278, 306, 416; Isabella, 416; James, 271, 283, 335, 370, 377, 426, 427.

MCGANNON, John, 308, 310, 357, 392.

461; Margaret, 366; Matthias, 448; Michael, 271, 323; Moles, 315; Nicholas, 448; William, 323, 456.

SOUTHER, Henry, 453; Stephen, 407.

SPARKS, William, 407.

SPILMAN, James, 322, 410, 467.

SPOTSWOOD, John, 435, 462, 464.

STANTON, Diana, 460; Lettice, 304, 314, 318, 361, 362, 393, 419; Richard, 298, 342, 384; Thomas, 304, 314, 318, 347, 361, 362, 372, 375, 393, 419, 450, 453, 455, 456, 461; William, 278, 460, 467.

STEPHENS, Winnifred, 274.

STEVENS, George, 372; James, 287, 339, 378, 383; Joseph, 281, 337, 415; Lewis, 278.

STEWART, Charles, 323, 398, 454; James, 323, 346, 348, 454; John, 296; Joseph, 447.

STORY, James, 314, 331.

STRINGFELLOW, George, 367, 432; Henry, 376, 379, 385, 458; William, 299, 342, 368, 380, 385.

STROTHER, Ann, 386; Anthony, 295, 310, 358,, 380, 418; Benjamin, 386, 406; Francis, 395, 430, 435, 451; French, 275, 279, 319, 403, 426, 441, 442, 451; George, 274; James, 275, 379; John, 300, 301, 308, 325, 333, 344, 352, 357, 362, 370, 386, 400, 421, 454, 468; Mary, 386; William, 432.

STUART, James, 318.

STUBBLEFIELD, George, 458; Thomas, 286, 339.

SUTHERLAND, John, 445.

SUTTON, Beaumont, 281, 303, 337, 387, 416.

SWINDLE, Michael, 275; Rebecca, 275; Timothy, 275.

TACKITT, John, 347, 348, 363.

TALIAFERRO, Peter, 462; Zachary, 339, 378, 427.

TAPP, Lewis, 406; William, 406.

TAYLOR, James, 471.

TERRELL, Robert, 454.

THOMAS, Benjamin, 306; Evan, 319, 376, 379; Edward, 406; John, 319, 462; Michael, 285, 318, 338, 378, 433; Richard, 285, 302, 345; William, 318, 440, 455.

THOMPSON, Catherine, 351, 390, 417; David, 342, 351, 384; Dekar, 298, 317, 329, 355, 381, 397, 398, 420 432, 445, 446.

THORNTON, Madam, 467.

THRELKELD, Henry, 346; Thomas, 286, 339, 378, 433; William, 397.

THURSTOUT, Aminadab, 355.

TILLMAN, John, 405, 426.

TINSLEY, Edward, 460.

TOWLES, Oliver, 285, 297, 315, 347, 355, 363, 376, 391, 418, 446, 459.

TURNER, Benjamin, 400; Edward,332; James, 354,386, 391; John, 354; John Baker, 287; Margaret, 355, 391, 417, 439; William, 298, 319, 329, 342, 354, 355, 356, 391, 403, 408, 412, 417, 423, 439.

TUTT, James, 283, 293; Richard, 283, 318, 355; William, 288, 295, 302, 318, 345, 355, 357, 387, 392.

TWENTYMAN, Benonie, 351, 357, 388, 392, 437.

TWYMAN, William, 328, 456.

TYLER, Francis, 273.

UNDERWOOD, Eleanor, 2 8 6, 339; Nathan, 328; Nathaniel, 456; Thomas, 319, 362, 367, 374; William, 286, 336, 339, 383, 411, 414.

UTZ, George, 307; Michael, 407.

VAWTER, David, 297, 298, 313, 342, 371, 384, 386, 401, 410, 412, 422, 432, 445, 449, 450; Richard, 433; William, 450.

VERNON, Richard, 295, 319, 383, 415, 456.

WAITE, John, 352, 390.

WALE, Thomas, 348.

WALKER, James, 313, 360, 405; John, 383; William, 271, 298, 308, 313, 323, 328, 330, 342, 371, 375, 384, 456, 472.

WALLE (Nalle), Francis, 300, 419; Isaac, 323; Jacob, 317, 318, 362. 419; Nanny, 318, 362, 419; William, 329, 400, 421, 425, 457.

WALLER, John, 348, 457.

WALLIS, John, 287, 289, 339, 368, 378, 429; Lewis, 300.

WARD, Jacob, 456.

WASHBURN, Lewis, 413.

WATKINS, Edmund, 395; Edward, 315, 319, 347, 380, 396, 397, 462; Richard, 399, 421. 429.

WATTS, Benjamin, 307, 408; John, 307; William, 451.

WAUGH, Alexander, 286, 416.

WAYLAND, Adam, 273, 276, 407, 447; John, 371.

WEAVER, John, 407; Matthias, 407; Peter, 407, 443.

WEEKLEY, John, 306.

WEEKS, Benjamin, 349, 388, 416.

WETHERALL, George, 275, 276, 278, 287, 308, 316, 339, 364,

370, 371, 378, 453, 463, 468; John, 275, 276, 308, 359, 381, Margaret, 275, 359, 381.

WHEATLEY, James, 455.

WHITE, Abbott, 300, 343; James, 427, 467; John, 409; William, 306, 376, 462.

WILDER, James, 326, 406; Peggy, 326.

WILHOIT, Adam, 371; John, 364; Margaret, 364.

WILLIAMS, James, 423, 449; John, 291, 329, 346, 404; Thomas, 403, 422; William, 272, 275, 278, 288, 289, 308, 311, 321, 332, 349, 370, 371, 387, 402, 409, 410, 414, 428, 442, 443, 448, 459, 465, 468, 471.

WILLIS, Elizabeth, 356, 378, 416, 425; John, 321, 387, 416; Lewis, 344, 411; William, 356, 387, 416, 425.

WINN, William, 363.

WINSLOW, Richard, 295, 383, 415.

WISEMAN, William, 347.

WITHERS, Thomas, 287.

WOODROE, Alexander, 322, 329, 330, 353, 354, 356, 366, 367, 391, 395, 409, 428, 440, 457.

WOOD, Joseph, 282, 283, 308, 370, 408, 459, 468.

WRIGHT, Alexander, 349, 393, 394, 419, 441; John, 401; Thomas, 400.

WYTHE, George, 273.

YANCEY, David, 310; Charles, 274, 347, 363; Elizabeth, 274; John, 273, 274, 282, 315, 337, 347, 424, 426; Lewis, 300, 319, 343, 346, 368, 376, 377, 379, 385, 396, 397, 425; Lewis Davis, 277, 306, 392, 356, 413; Richard, 297,

www.ingramcontent.com/pod-product-compliance
Lightning Source LLC
Chambersburg PA
CBHW021838020426
42334CB00014B/690